# Changing Lives in Appalachia
## The NEW OPPORTUNITY SCHOOL for WOMEN

by
Jane B. Stephenson

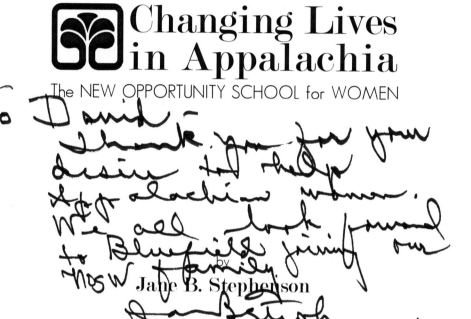

**JSF**
JESSE STUART
FOUNDATION
Ashland, Kentucky
2013

CHANGING LIVES Copyright © 2013 by Jane B. Stephenson

All rights reserved. Printed in the United States of America. No part of this publication may be reproduced in whole or in part, or utilized in any form or by any means, electronic or mechanical, including photocopying, recording, or by any information or retrieval system, without written permission of the publisher.

ISBN: 978-1-938471-18-6

Published by

**JSF**
JESSE STUART
FOUNDATION

1645 Winchester Avenue
Ashland, Kentucky 41101
(606) 326-1667
jsfbooks.com

# Changing Lives in Appalachia
## The NEW OPPORTUNITY SCHOOL for WOMEN

**About the cover:** The cover image is a story quilt created by the Berea New Opportunity School for Women, class of 2012, led by Deborah Hille and quilted by Joanne Grimes. The expressive arts curriculum was created at the Lees-McRae College NOSW and is used at all NOSW locations. Designing quilt squares helps empower the participants and increase their sense of competency as the women explore their personal stories to create a shared story in the form of a quilt. In addition, it creates a visual record of their unique contributions to NOSW as a gift to the school and future participants. Participants are asked to visualize an image that is representative of themselves and their history. It can be an image of the transformation they are undergoing at NOSW, something they want to let go of or hold on to, an image of the true self, or a particular story that represents each individual. This exceptional quilt was also designed to celebrate the twenty-fifth anniversary of the NOSW—Berea. (Photo credits: David Stephenson and Doug Pratt)

# TABLE of CONTENTS

DEDICATION. . . . . . . . . . . . . . . . . . . . . . . . . . . . . . . . . . . . . . . . . vi
PREFACE. . . . . . . . . . . . . . . . . . . . . . . . . . . . . . . . . . . . . . . . . . . vii

PART I: LIFE STORIES . . . . . . . . . . . . . . . . . . . . . . . . . . . . . . . . .1
    Introduction . . . . . . . . . . . . . . . . . . . . . . . . . . . . . . . . . . . . . . .2
    Alma . . . . . . . . . . . . . . . . . . . . . . . . . . . . . . . . . . . . . . . . . . . . .3
    Erin . . . . . . . . . . . . . . . . . . . . . . . . . . . . . . . . . . . . . . . . . . . . .10
    Garnet . . . . . . . . . . . . . . . . . . . . . . . . . . . . . . . . . . . . . . . . . . .15
    George Ann. . . . . . . . . . . . . . . . . . . . . . . . . . . . . . . . . . . . . . .21
    Mary . . . . . . . . . . . . . . . . . . . . . . . . . . . . . . . . . . . . . . . . . . . .27
    Shirley . . . . . . . . . . . . . . . . . . . . . . . . . . . . . . . . . . . . . . . . . . .31
    Sadie . . . . . . . . . . . . . . . . . . . . . . . . . . . . . . . . . . . . . . . . . . . .35

PART II: THE PROGRAM. . . . . . . . . . . . . . . . . . . . . . . . . . . . . . .39
    The Women of the New Opportunity School . . . . . . . . . . . . . . .40
    The Three-Week Experience. . . . . . . . . . . . . . . . . . . . . . . . . . .58
    The Results . . . . . . . . . . . . . . . . . . . . . . . . . . . . . . . . . . . . . . .86

PART III: TWENTY-FIVE YEARS OF HISTORY . . . . . . . . . . . . . . . .91
    In the Beginning. . . . . . . . . . . . . . . . . . . . . . . . . . . . . . . . . . . .92
    New Paths. . . . . . . . . . . . . . . . . . . . . . . . . . . . . . . . . . . . . . .117
    Leading the New Opportunity School Into the Future . . . . . . .133

APPENDIX . . . . . . . . . . . . . . . . . . . . . . . . . . . . . . . . . . . . . . . .151

# DEDICATION

We are saddened by the loss of twenty-five graduates of the New Opportunity School over these twenty-five years. This book is dedicated to their memory as well as the memory of other people who have played a crucial role in the New Opportunity School through the years:

John B. Stephenson
Sidney Farr
Alex Haley

Wilma Dykeman
Rudy Abramson
Bob Sexton

## GRAPHICS

GRADUATES

Donna Adams
Mary Fran Adams
Judy Allen
Janice Bell
Wilma (Libby) Chenault
Kathy Cornett
Cathy Ferrell
Berta Gayle
Barbara Gipson
Joann Mitchell Hall
Janice Homuth
Robbie Jones

Yvonne Jones
Gaye Killin
Emma Angel McIntire
Sue Moore
Donna Napier
Daphne Olson
Wanda Purkey
Alice Ryan
Sonja Rogers
Millie Rodden
Gloria Snyder
Beulah Ward

Brenda Willis

# PREFACE

A child of Appalachia, I grew up in the beautiful, rural mountains of North Carolina. My home county of Avery was the newest, and smallest with the lowest per capita income in the state. As I remember my childhood, it seemed everyone worked hard, and the children had the freedom to roam the mountains and valleys without fear. Early on, however, I learned that boys had more advantages than girls with a long list of *don'ts* for girls but not for boys. I remember thinking how unfair that was. It was a given that I would go to college, but my choices of occupations were limited to teacher, nurse, or secretary. Girls were told they didn't need to learn math or economics or any of the hard sciences or the languages of commerce. Some of us were told we should go to college only because we might need a skill to "fall back on," in case our marriages failed!

When moving to Kentucky in the mid-1960s, I was not surprised to learn that girls in Kentucky Appalachia (fifty-four of the 120 counties as defined by the Appalachian Regional Commission) were still being expected to marry young, have children, and staying in school wasn't a high priority. Moving to Berea in 1984 allowed me to meet more rural women and learn of their plight and their desire for a better life. I felt "called" to find a way to help the women I met and got to know.

Being at the right place at the right time was a divinely led opportunity; one that brought forth the resources necessary to create the miracle of the New Opportunity School for Women (NOSW) I founded in 1987. Over the years, I have watched the miraculous changes in the lives of our participants. I realize I have only been an instrument in bringing life and growth to this special program. The late Alex Haley, a supporter of our program, said, "If you see a turtle sitting on a fence post, you know he had help getting there." That's the story of the NOSW. The assistance needed to make the NOSW a reality and to continue these twenty-five years has come from hundreds of devoted people.

The twenty-seven graduates who agreed to tell their stories are the focus of this book. They have overcome terrible hardships as children and adults, and many have endured emotional and physical harm from people in their lives. Their stories are often painful for them to relate and difficult to capture in words.

These women overcame fear to leave home, family, and friends, to travel a new journey to the New Opportunity Schools in Berea, Kentucky, and in Banner Elk, North Carolina. They came seeking better lives for themselves and their children. Though lacking self-confidence, these women found child-care providers, and made transportation arrangements (which might mean riding a bus for hours). They convinced husbands, boyfriends, mothers, children, and other relatives and friends that they must attend this three-week residential school. As you read their stories, you will admire their courage and accomplishments, and feel elation for the progress they have made toward more productive and fulfilling lives.

The NOSW is a unique program. It is designed to build the confidence of the participants and provide new ideas, cultural opportunities, and job search skills, while instilling the desire for more education and training. We have seen the results: lives changed, families who now believe education is vital, and improved family economic circumstances. The reward is watching our graduates get good jobs with benefits and medical care for their families for the very first time. We continue to celebrate the women who have, over a period of years, found ways to work toward college degrees; some even receiving master's degrees. This book is not only about NOSW graduates who have changed their lives but it is also about their children, friends, and other family members who have been inspired to make positive change in their lives as well. As one graduate, Garnet, said, "I found myself again through the God-inspired NOSW program."

Our work is destined to continue beyond these twenty-five years, even after an arsonist destroyed our Berea office in December 2011. Preparations have begun for another NOSW site opening in 2013 on the border of Virginia and West Virginia at Bluefield College. This new site will allow even more courageous Appalachian women to become part of the NOSW family in the years ahead and benefit from the knowledge and experience gained during the three-week sessions.

I am grateful to my late husband, John Stephenson, for encouraging me to start the NOSW and for supporting the program in many different ways from 1987 until his untimely death in 1994. I am grateful to my children and grandchildren, who have always understood my passion for the NOSW and have continuously been supportive: David, Angie, and Tory; Rebecca and Barry; Jennifer, Brooks, Jonathan, and Cullen. I am also thankful for the many donors, friends, foundations, civic groups, churches, instructors, internship supervisors, and especially the staff and board members of our two schools who have cared for and supported the NOSW.

I thank the many people who have helped with the birth of this book through their constant encouragement, reading and editing, providing great suggestions, and listening to my thoughts and fears: Jim Gifford and Suzanna Stephens of the Jesse Stuart Foundation; Gurney Norman; Frank Taylor; Ben Poage; Angie Stephenson; Leslie Guttman; members of Neil Chethik's nonfiction writing group at the Carnegie Center; David Stephenson for his patience explaining to his mother time-saving ways to "fix things" on my computer when I made mistakes and especially for his help with photograph selections for this book; Debbie King, who cheerfully searched for NOSW information in her computer files; Lori Sliwa and Karen Sabo, executive directors of our two sites, and the NOSW staff and board members at both locations; photographers David Stephenson, Michael Joslin, Meghan Wright, and Mike Nichols for recording so many wonderful activities of the NOSW that are featured in this book; the First Christian Church of Berea, who gave us a place to continue our work after the fire; and my patient constant companion, "Charlie-dog."

Most importantly, I again thank the twentyy-seven women who agreed to tell their stories for this book. To the 685 graduates of the combined Kentucky and North Carolina programs, we honor you for your courage and your accomplishments. As a recent graduate said, "We will now reach to the stars, even if we have to stand on a cactus to do so." That's the spirit of the New Opportunity School!

*Jane B. Stephenson*, Founder
New Opportunity School for Women

# Part I
# LIFE STORIES

## INTRODUCTION

The lives of the women included here are varied. They have shared intimate details of their lives. You will read about sexual abuse, drug and alcohol abuse, and in the case of Mary, understand what life is like for a refugee who settled in these mountains. The NOSW's mission is to improve lives of Appalachian women. Many women who have been in the NOSW were originally from outside the region but came to Appalachia to marry, or had other family members who settled here and followed them. They became Appalachians, and wanted to learn more about their adopted homes and, for a variety of reasons, needed the programs of the NOSW. We are grateful they have shared their stories with us.

While this book was still in the "thinking stage," I knew I wanted to include life stories written by the women who had graduated from the NOSW. Their stories are so important and who can tell them better than they can?

I sent a letter to all graduates of the NOSW from the Berea and Lees-McRae College programs, asking that anyone willing to send their story to me to please do so. I was thrilled that twenty-seven women responded, thoughtfully sharing and opening their lives to all of us. I am thankful and grateful to these women. You will find them listed in the appendix of this book. Several women asked that their real names not be used and I have respected their wishes and an asterisk is placed beside their assumed names in the appendix list.

All the women agreed I could use my judgment in how I presented their stories, including editing, making them shorter or placing them in a sequence to make for easier reading.

Although only seven complete stories are shared in the following section, the other twenty women are quoted extensively in Part II of this book. Their quotes have added enormously to the story of the New Opportunity School, and I thank each one personally.

# ALMA

***"If the land was parchment and the sea was ink I could still never write all the ways the NOSW changed my life."***
                                                                – **Alma**

As I look back on my life, I can't perceive that I'm over a half-century old. This is hard to comprehend as it was only a few years ago, on a hot August morning on a hill called Fairview, in a small mining town of Hitchins, Kentucky, that I was born—or, as the saying goes in our family, "I was hatched."

Even more miraculous was that there were two of me. My twin's name was Thelma. She passed away soon after being born. Part of me still wonders what fun we could have had had she lived. The Lord called her home so Mom dressed her in a doll's dress to be laid out. The dress fit her to a T because together, we weighed as much as a five-pound bag of sugar. The loss of one child was bad enough for any woman, but Mom was told that if something wasn't done fast I would soon follow Thelma to be with the angels. As Mom held me close to her heart, she made a heart-wrenching decision: she had other children who needed her. After a long, weary night of prayer and worry, Mom knew what she had to do. She sent for my grandfather and his new wife. I was given to them to be raised.

Grandpa worked at the General-RECF Actors Brickyard in Hitchins. He had a good job with hospitalization. I was put into a hospital for thirty days and was in an incubator—like a baby chick. The days were touch-and-go because in 1953, the chances for a preemie were slim. I beat the odds and eventually came home to my new family.

Six wonderful years flew by. On a warm May day, as the birds were singing and the flowers blooming in the garden she loved, my grandmother flew away with the angels. All my lessons about Jesus and the Bible were over. The walks in the woods, the bedtime stories, everything—gone. Once again, I was alone.

Two weeks later, my world changed again. Grandpa sold our house. We moved to a five-room house with no running water or bathroom. Of course, back then, no one had a bathroom—only a path out back. It was in a swampy area, and over the years we lived there we lost everything we owned five times to floods. Grandpa, not knowing how to raise a little girl, cut off my hair and put me in boy's jeans and shirts, which was what I wore until I was eighteen when a nice neighbor lady gave me some hand-me-downs.

Life with Grandpa was hard. In the summer we raised a garden and canned food for winter. In the winter there was always wood and coal to get in. Grandpa left me alone a lot when he went coon hunting, so after chores were done in summer, I headed for the hills I loved so well. The only contact with the outside world was when I went to school. There was no one to interact with, so for company I talked to the animals in the woods. The animals were my family. I imagined I was queen of the forest and the animals my subjects, from the newts in the pond to the bobcat in the coal mine. I had another group of friends—my books. I could read about other places and people, and I could be right there doing what they were doing.

We lived on Grandpa's Social Security check, and it wasn't much. We trapped and hunted squirrels, rabbits, and quail. I would never let him hunt in the woods around where we lived because those animals were my friends. Sometimes, we went around to stores in Grayson and got their day-old meat and food to feed to our coonhounds. We would place it in the creek in a tin box Grandpa fixed for that purpose. There were a few winters when we would go and get the meat out of the box, scrap off the mold, fry it up, and eat it ourselves.

Most summers I lived in the smokehouse, where I had made myself a zoo lab where I did experiments. I was doing "scientific research," mostly watching tadpoles become frogs. One time, I took the heart of a squirrel we had cleaned and hooked it to a cooper wire connected to a battery. Then I put the wire in the squirrel's heart and it beat a few times. I had made a defibrillator and didn't even know it!

I loved school. There, my thirst for knowledge was fed at warp speed. The most important day in school was when I was in the sixth grade and a teacher arrived that I loved from then to now. He was an art teacher and the most handsome man I had ever seen. He was my knight in shining armor. He opened a world of art and beauty to me that no one can ever take away. Even though he was killed in 1998 in a car wreck, in my heart he will live on forever.

Let's fast-forward to when I married Jim Young. We had a paper route for the Ashland newspaper. We had the route about three years when he come in one evening and asked for a divorce. I gave him a divorce and left to live on a farm in a place called Wolfpen. I took care of the farm animals and kept an eye on things. I worked in the tobacco fields. One evening, an Army recruiter came by asking for directions. We got to talking and she told me if I lost some weight, I could join the Army. At age thirty-four, I did.

I flew to Fort Jackson, South Carolina, where I spent nine weeks. I worked from four a.m. to one p.m. I learned everything from how to fire an M16 to how to live off the land. We got a few day's leave to go home for Christmas and while on leave I married Jim Young again.

Before graduation from basic training, we got to crawl in mud under barbed wire while live shells were going off all around us. To top it off, the cadre were in towers shooting live rounds over our heads as we made our way to safety. To this day I tell myself, "You got through basic training for the Army so there is nothing you cannot do when you set your mind to it."

After basic training, I was sent to Redstone, Alabama, where I finished up my training in six weeks. After that I was sent to Germany to take up my duties as an ammunitions specialist. I had been there about six months and was getting ready to move off base and send for Jim, when we had a lockdown. Then I learned the Red Cross was trying to reach me to tell me that Jim had had a massive heart attack and was in the ICU in a hospital in Ashland, Kentucky. I was on the next flight to the USA. I got reassigned to Fort Knox, Kentucky, and was promised a permanent post. Jim got out of the hospital and we moved to Fort Knox, but eventually, I left the Army and joined the Army Reserve in Huntington, West Virginia.

After I got off active duty, we came back home to Carter County, Kentucky. For the first four months we slept in our car. Then I received my last check from the Army, and I bought a trailer shell and moved it to a rented lot. We fixed it up enough to live in, but it had no running water or electricity. We were out of the weather and warm and dry. I learned to be thankful for whatever you have because you could lose it all in one sweep of fate. Even when things are low, you can always find a bright spot. There's a saying I heard once that has helped me so many times: "I complained I had no shoes until I met a man that had no feet." No matter how bad things get, they could always be worse.

I looked and looked for work. Soon there was no money to even be able to keep the car. We had to walk everywhere. Our life was like this for about two years. Then one of the most important days of my life came. I learned I had been accepted to the New Opportunity School for Women.

Like most special events in our lives, the day started out very routine. I had walked all day asking for work and still had three miles to go till I was home. The cold March wind was blowing inside my nylon jacket like a big balloon. To warm myself, I stopped at a local restaurant to get a glass of water and a packet of lemon juice so I could fix myself a poor man's lemonade. I spied a newspaper on the next table, so while waiting for my water, I began to read. It was like neon letters that I read about the New Opportunity School for Women in Berea, Kentucky. The more I read the more hope came into my heart and mind that maybe I could go. As I drank my water, more and more ideas came to mind about how I would get to Berea if I was accepted. I placed the ad in my coat pocket, and all the way home I would put my hand in my pocket to feel the ad to make sure it wasn't a dream. That evening, while getting water out of the spring, I lifted my eyes toward heaven and asked for help to get to go to Berea. I was all alone. Jim was out spending time with his drinking buddies, as he did a lot now. I placed the ad under my pillowcase. I went to sleep on my pallet on the floor as the cold air was warmed by the kerosene heater and I dreamed of going to Berea.

The next morning I was out the door at daybreak, walking into town. I had a plan in my heart and mind. The first part of my plan was to go to the Carter County Courthouse and speak to my friend, Mr. Bill Woods, who was the district judge. I asked him for help and showed him the ad. He read it and said if I was accepted, he would personally take me to Berea. He wrote me a letter of recommendation. Then I left to find a cousin, Verla Wilcox, to ask her for a letter, too. She helped me fill out the application and drove me to the Grayson Post Office. With a prayer, I mailed the letter and application.

Life went back to reality, and I worked some here and there. I was feeling all hope was gone when I heard from Jane Stephenson, and learned that I was accepted by the New Opportunity School. I didn't walk home, I floated.

If the land was parchment and the sea was ink, I could still never write all the ways the NOSW changed my life. First, I remember how I learned to use a computer. Now I own a new Windows 7 computer. My work assignment at the NOSW was at facilities management at Berea College where I learned to put information in a computer.

There were so many firsts in my time at Berea. For example, going to the Cincinnati Art Museum that I had only heard about from my wonderful art teacher. I bought me a little glass dragon there. Every time I look at the dragon, I laugh as I remember the good day I had at the museum. Another memory is the meals at the Boone Tavern Hotel. The first meal I ate there was odd, as I had never seen so many knives and forks at one place setting. I looked around to see who I was supposed to share them with and was totally shocked to learn that they were all for me as the different courses were served. I felt like a queen.

The self-esteem class was another life-changing class. That was the first time I had ever heard of such a thing called self-esteem. I learned I was a human being and not a weird mistake or alien from another planet. I had worth and could help myself and others to feel good about themselves.

There were so many other classes that were taught by wonderful people and meant so much to me. I learned so much and still think of the experience often.

When I came home after the three weeks at the NOSW, I learned my landlord had sold the rented lot my trailer was on. A neighbor let me set my trailer on his land, but things went from bad to worse. Jim was drinking more so we broke up again. I sold the trailer and moved to a town where I got a job as a security guard at Cook's Meat Plant. I worked there about a year, then I moved into the apartment where I have lived for the last seventeen years.

During this time, I was given a scholarship from the NOSW so I could take classes at Ashland Community College. Oh the joy I experienced by being part of that higher institution of learning, which thrilled me to my very core. Then I received a scholarship to go full-time, which I did until my car died. I planned to go back to school but I still haven't gotten to go back to college. Take it from me, if you get a gift of learning like that, don't waste it by saying you will do it tomorrow, for sometimes, tomorrow never comes.

Later on, I met a gentleman named Thurston. He had a booth at the Carter County Flea Market. I helped him in his shop for the six years we were engaged. I learned a lot about inventory, displays, serving customers. Then we broke up and I got a part-time job in a VA hospital in Huntington, West Virginia. I loved my work but I started to get real sick. It seemed like every week I was in the ER. I was there twenty-eight times, and it was like I was going to die. I lost almost sixty pounds. Finally it was found that my gallbladder wasn't working. It was taken out, and it took me a year to get back on my feet. I was told I could come back to work at the VA Hospital. I was really happy!

Then on the first evening before I was to go back to work, I stopped to get gas for the next day. I had just gotten out of my car to pay when out of nowhere a Blazer hit me. I fell to the pavement. My head bounced off the ground. Fortunately, a school nurse was there who talked to me to try to keep me from going into shock. When I woke up in the hospital, all I could think was that now I couldn't go back to work. It took months before I recovered from this act of fate.

I am still hanging in there. My faith in the Lord and the lessons I learned at the NOSW have served me well. I am always telling everyone I meet about my Lord, Jesus, and I tell the women I meet that the NOSW will change your life and that no matter where you are in your life, the NOSW can take you to new places you never dreamed of.

# ERIN

*"I have hope: hope for life today, hope for myself."*
—**Erin**

My name is Erin and I am an addict. This is my story.

I was raised in southwest Virginia, and for as long as I can remember I never felt like I fit in or measured up. I felt like an outsider. I felt I was ugly inside and out. From a very young age, I compared myself to other people and always came up short. My younger sister is petite and beautiful. I am tall and thick with big hands and feet. I envied her and wanted to be her so badly.

Even in childhood, I had addictive tendencies. I loved food and ate a lot. I always wanted more. I continued loathing myself into adolescence. The grunge era was in and it fascinated me. I did not feel connected with "normal" people. They did not understand.

I had a good childhood and a loving family. Nobody suspected that I was dying inside. I can remember staring out my bedroom window waiting for someone to save me. I would cut myself. I was never brave enough to cut deep. I liked feeling the pain—it made me feel alive.

I started drinking somewhere around the age of eleven or twelve. The first time I smoked marijuana I was thirteen. I loved it. By fifteen I had done cocaine numerous times and tried LSD. I continued to smoke pot and drink. I thought the people I was running around with were the cool crowd, but I still felt like I was on the outside looking in. At sixteen I was introduced to prescription pain meds, like Oxycontin and Lortab. At first they made me sick, but it was what people were doing and I liked the numbness they instilled.

I did well in high school. I got good grades and played sports. I used some sort of substance every day but I wasn't hooked yet. I graduated in 2001 and that following fall moved to Radford, Virginia, to attend Radford University.

I went to college because it was the right thing to do. I really didn't know what I wanted to do, so I just picked a major, elementary education, and stuck with it. I got good grades most semesters. But deep down I was terrified. The people there intimidated me. I was afraid to get drunk at parties. I was afraid to get close to anyone. During my junior year I came back home and moved in with my boyfriend. I was abusing prescription meds again. This time I became dependent. I had to have them or I felt terrible.

In 2003, I got pregnant. I was both excited and scared. I was nineteen and continued to use drugs even though I knew I should stop. I wanted to stop but I couldn't. They were all around me.

A few months into my pregnancy, I had a miscarriage. I blamed myself. I hated myself. I knew it was all my fault. To cope, I used more and more, and drugs became what I had to have to function and feel normal. I had to use as soon as I woke up and throughout the day, every day. All my money went for that next high.

I moved near Radford with a new boyfriend. I attempted school but didn't have any money and needed to feed my habit every day. In January 2005, I had had enough. I was broke, broken, and exhausted. I quit using pills. I still drank and smoked pot some. But in my mind, I was doing well.

I got pregnant again and moved back to my hometown and got married. (I had quit school.) In October, my son was born. He was so beautiful, so perfect. He was my everything, but even my son could not make me feel whole. My doctor wrote me prescriptions for pain. Before I knew it, I was hooked again. My husband was also using and we didn't want to share. This drove us apart and we separated. I was so numb that I didn't really care.

I continued to use heavily, even taking my son with me on my hunt for more drugs. He would be in a car seat all day long while I drove the roads searching for ways to get more drugs. I took him to some really sketchy places.

Then I met a man with perfect qualifications: He was prescribed lots of meds and knew where to get even more. We moved in together, but I would leave for days and weeks at a time with different guys to do more drugs. I didn't care about anyone but myself.

In August 2007 I got pregnant once again. My boyfriend and I eloped. I didn't tell my parents until afterward. I attempted a so-called normal life, which meant keeping my drug use to a minimum. Controlled drug use for an active addict is torture. It is living hell, second only to withdrawal.

My husband wanted me to quit, but even pregnancy couldn't keep me clean. I tried—God knows I tried. I sat up night after night watching the shadows on the walls. I ached and jerked and sweated. I would rub Icy Hot all over my body. I was miserable. I had to have drugs. I was dying without them.

I gave in. My husband would catch me using, and in a fit of rage, would hit me. I hated myself for using drugs; I hated him for trying to force me to stop. He would take my keys and my phone. When he would leave, I would walk to the gas station, use the pay phone, and someone would bring me what I needed.

The birth of my second son was bittersweet. Before he was born, I had gone to the doctor for a routine checkup, but I snorted dope before my appointment. When they did the stress test, the baby did not move. Of course, this raised concern. It never even crossed my mind that they would test me for drugs. They admitted me to the hospital and continued the stress test. I continued to use drugs while in the hospital. Of course, I failed the test and was found out. I was induced and my son was born. He was so beautiful but was dependent on the meds I was taking. He squirmed and cried the high-pitch squeal of addicted babies. He lost weight and didn't sleep well. I knew I had hurt him.

The abuse from my husband persisted, and after a particularly bad fight I left him to live with my parents. I didn't stay with them long as I met a man who promised to rescue me. He was the most abusive man I have ever encountered. I cheated on him. I lied to him.

We would fight violently. He would always win. I was too afraid to commit suicide but I was slowly killing myself with drugs.

My parents quit helping me because of my substance abuse. I remember my mother telling me through tears, "I took up for you." I hated that I hurt her, but not enough to stop. Without the help of my family, I had to resort to other means. I wrote books of bad checks, took out payday loans I had no intention of paying, and stole money and drugs. I was working until I got charged with embezzlement. In February 2009, I was admitted to a psych ward in Princeton, West Virginia. I agreed to sign myself in for a seventy-two-hour observation. They put me on Klonodin for withdrawal. I slept most of the time. However, I was released since they were not a detox center.

I lost custody of my children. I was a danger to myself and those around me. I was charged with stealing my parents' credit cards and found myself sitting in jail. I was indicted with fourteen felonies and three misdemeanors. I had no idea when I would be coming home. Then I learned I was being referred for an intensive treatment program, but I wanted nothing to do with it. However in October 2009, I went to the New Beginnings treatment program and was there for ninety days.

In treatment I learned about addiction as a disease. I had no idea I was sick or that there were others like me. I am a sick person trying to get well—not a bad person trying to get good. I was taught the twelve-step program. The staff told me I didn't have to get high anymore and to never forget where I came from. It began to make sense. I was no longer alone. I still felt unworthy of love, but somewhere along the way I found a conscious contact with the God of my understanding.

I came home from treatment in January, 2010. I was scared to death but happy. I was clean! I didn't have to lie and steal and cheat any more. I felt contentment for the first time in my life.

Staying clean is not easy. Learning to live is a struggle. Life is better today. Recovery is a process. If I can accept others and life as it is, I am more content. The world doesn't change; I do.

But after getting clean, I still didn't have a job; I wasn't going to school. I was trying to get out of an abusive relationship. I needed help learning how to live. I learned about the New Opportunity School for Women at Lees-McRae College and applied. I was thrilled when I was accepted. I went there feeling very unsure but I left with confidence, self-esteem, and self-respect. I now believe I can turn my life around and that I deserve good things and happiness.

Today, I have many blessings in my life. I have joint custody of my children and see them every other weekend. My goal is to have my children in my home again.

I have hope: hope for life today, hope for myself. I have real, true friends and a good relationship with my parents. I have a job that is perfect for me. I am back in school to get my bachelor's in human services. Then I am going to get my master's degree in substance abuse counseling.

That's the plan for now; more will be revealed to me!

## GARNET
### My Story: Out of the Woods

*"Thanks to the New Opportunity School for Women, I can provide the same hope, empowerment, and motivation to the women I am privileged to serve, helping them to successfully navigate the journey 'out of the woods'."*

**—Garnet**

It is hard to believe now that I am the same person who was in Berea twenty-one years ago at the New Opportunity School for Women in January 1991. I could never have predicted how great an effect that three-week experience would have on my life. It was a real turning point for me. I had another turning point in my life when I was about twelve-years-old that resulted in me losing myself for over twenty-five years. But I found myself again through the God-inspired New Opportunity School for Women program.

I grew up in southeastern Kentucky, one of seven children. My family was very poor. We lived on thirty-three dollars a month from welfare and "commodities" (powdered milk, yellow cornmeal, and powdered eggs, mostly) that were given out monthly twenty miles away from our holler. It would take Daddy and Mommy all day (from before daylight until after dark) to get into town, stand in line, and carry the commodities back in burlap bags. We had a cow for milk, raised a couple of hogs a year for meat, and grew a garden. We didn't have much in the way of material possessions, but we were rich in ways that I am only now aware of. Of course, like a lot of families that I see today, we had our vices—which kept us locked in a cycle of poverty and sometimes violence. My Daddy would get drunk at least once a month, drag out an old gun and raise hell. Mommy would take us kids and hide in the hills till he passed out or sobered up. These drunkfests were not unusual occurrences, and we pretty much took it in stride.

My first memories involve my family being stalked by a welfare worker who would come up through the creek and across briars and through the brushes to try to catch my Daddy working in the garden. Daddy was a disabled coal miner who was legally blind, with black lung disease and severe back problems from his years of crawling around in the mines. He would prop himself up on a homemade cane and try to hoe in the garden. Some of us kids would stay posted to watch for Mrs. T and sound the alarm.

I was a "middle child," which meant I was more or less invisible, at least to Daddy and Mommy. I lived in my head and had a great imagination. We kids spent a lot of time running around in the mountains. I thought life was just a wonderful adventure! The scariest and maybe the worst day of my life was the first day of school. I was excited because it was a new experience; we rarely ever left the holler so I did not have much of an idea about what life was like "out there." I soon found out. One of my first lessons was to find out that being poor was something to be ashamed of. I wasn't sure why, but it must have been because we were "bad." It was an adjustment to my world view, but I did survive. I loved learning. However, I admit that reading about Tom, Jane, and Jip running around on sidewalks in cute little clothes and jumping puddles in red galoshes and raincoats seemed to be in the realm of science fiction. My older brother and sister had already taught me to read so that got me into a great deal of trouble as well. We were reading Zane Grey westerns by the time we were six- or seven-years-old. We would steal books from Daddy and sneak out in the barn and read.

My Daddy only went to the third grade and Mommy said she went to the eighth. I found out years later that she had only made it through fifth grade. My Dad could read, though, and loved books. He wore thick glasses and would sit with a magnifying glass and try to read. When I think about it now, it was so sad. He had almost completely lost his eyesight by the time he was fifty-years-old. His corrected vision was 20/200 in one eye, and he was completely blind in the other. I heard a story once about him that broke my heart and stuck in my mind. He was only thirteen-years-old when he started working in the coal mines. He was fifteen when he got married and had his first child. His first wife (not my mother) got upset when she went to the "company store" to "draw down scrip," and there was no money in the account. Back in those days, the miners made about a dollar a day, but were paid with money minted by the mine owners themselves. The money had to be spent in the company-owned stores. They usually spent it faster than they could make it, so families were so deep in debt that they could never "escape" the system. The mine owners owned the houses, the stores, and the men.

Anyway, Daddy's wife (who was twelve-years-old at the time), thinking he was "fooling around" with another woman, followed Daddy one day. He turned off the path before he got to the mine entrance and went up into the woods. He had a book hidden in a log back there and had been spending his days sneaking off and reading. He caught hell, but I am sure he thought it was worth it! I inherited my love of reading from him. Most of the adventures that I had in my young life came from books, but then I "forgot" how to read and how to live for many years as I moved into the world of a teenage girl-woman.

The turning point in my life came at age twelve when I had the highest grades in my seventh grade class and won the honor of participating in the eighth grade graduation. But I was asked by a teacher and two of my classmates to let one of the other girls in the class do it "because you have to wear a nice dress and perfume."

Still believing that I could "be somebody," I refused to step aside. My mommy bought me a horrid yellow dress at a secondhand store. The dress was too tight and definitely inappropriate. I was ashamed of myself and could barely get through my short speech. It was such a devastating experience that I walked outside to breathe and try to gather what was left of my pride. I was standing there in mortification when some older guys drove by, whistled, and blew the horn at me.

All of a sudden I was beautiful and worthy. It was a downhill slide after that. I was pregnant at sixteen, dropped out of school, went on welfare, married my first husband at seventeen (a thirty-two-year-old total varmint), married again at eighteen to an abusive alcoholic, and again at twenty-five to my third husband. I thought if I could find the right man everything would be OK. I had been told that success was finding a man to take care of you.

Well, it wasn't. I did settle down and tried to raise my two children. I hoped that my kids would be able to have a life that I had not had a chance to have. I was miserable, lost, and lonely for many years. We were very poor. My husband could barely make enough money to buy groceries and pay the utilities. In January 1991, I was still washing clothes on the back porch in a wringer washer and staying one step ahead of the cut-off man. I was determined that my children would have more, would be more. My son could have qualified for a scholarship in art, but he was determined to go to work in the coal mines. He did make it through high school, but it was a battle with him and with my family who didn't care about education. Out of the original seven of us children, only one, my oldest brother, graduated high school. All of us girls dropped out at sixteen. My husband had only completed the eighth grade.

When my daughter turned sixteen, she absolutely refused to go to school. I saw her life going exactly the way mine, my mother's, and my sisters' lives had all gone. I was thirty-seven-years-old and felt the same sense of shame that I had felt as a child. I was devastated. My husband and I were having serious arguments and fighting all the time over money, over our families, over anything and nothing. I was literally suicidal. For real, I asked God to either help me or kill me. I felt trapped in my own head and tired of the everyday struggle to survive. I went downstairs one night after my husband and children had gone to sleep and sat down at the kitchen table in total despair. There was a newspaper on the table. A paragraph seemed to jump off the page. One paragraph that changed my life.

"The New Opportunity School for Women between the ages of 30 and 55 who are at a turning point in their lives…" I called the number on the advertisement and the rest is history.

I got to go back to school! I completed my undergraduate degree and then worked on getting my master's degree in social work while I was working with a community mental health center. I have worked for the past sixteen years as a professional counselor. I am now working with a program through a university where I have been employed for the past eight years. I work primarily with women referred through the Department for Community Based Services Cabinet for Families and Children (the modern-day welfare system). The goal of the program is to assist low-income women and families to become self-sufficient and overcome barriers, especially substance abuse, intimate partner violence (domestic violence), mental health issues, and learning problems. I am able to use much of my own life experience, as well as my education and professional experience/ expertise, to help other women struggling with poverty (and the many manifestations of poverty).

I owe most (if not all) of this success to the New Opportunity School for Women. The program was designed for me. One of the first requirements of the program was to read several books that were mailed to us. I had never read or seen Appalachian literature. I would sit on the porch, watching the wringer washer grind and slosh, and read about other women just like me, women who thought like me, felt like me, grew up like me. Before I even left for the three-week program, I had started to see beyond the horizon of entrapment.

By the time I came back home, I was not ashamed of being me, of being poor. I was proud of my daddy who worked almost forty years in the coal mines before he was fifty-years-old to make a few greedy "outsiders" rich. I was proud of my mother, who had raised seven children by literally digging sustenance from the ground.

Although I grew up in the 1950s and 1960s, and it is now 2012, many of the women I work with have backgrounds similar to mine.

Thanks to the New Opportunity School for Women, I can provide the same hope, empowerment, and motivation to the women I am privileged to serve, helping them to successfully navigate the journey "out of the woods."

## GEORGE ANN

*"I had yearned and longed for education all my life, and for the first time, I knew I was capable of getting the education that had been denied to me for so long."*

—George Ann

I was born in White Oak Holler in my mom's parents' home. From there, we moved to Greene Cove Holler where my dad's parents lived along with many aunts, uncles, and cousins. My dad and grandfather had the same name: George. I guess they thought I was going to be a boy. That's where I got the name George. I grew up believing my name was Georgia, but I was nicknamed Susie. I truly never knew what my true name was until I moved to Kentucky and filled out tax papers and listed my name as Georgia. They had no record of me.

Growing up, I was taught that girls were to be "seen and not heard." There was sexual abuse from several kinfolk to me and my sister, Virginia. However, back then you did not say a word, or you would have been called a liar and scorned from the community. In my mind, I was still a virgin because the sexual abuse did not involve penetration.

When I was still a kid, I remember how my Dad liked guns and would not hesitate to use them if he thought someone was trying to hurt him. He did not realize the damage he was doing to us young children at the time. Even though we were related to most everyone in the holler, we were still the "outcasts" because we were always running from my Dad when he was drinking and my mom was fearful—and still is, even though she is ninety-years-old.

I can remember walking those gravel roads in pitch-black dark to a neighbor's house at least a mile away. My dad was trying to hit Mom with steel knocks, and my sister was getting in between them and telling Daddy to go ahead and hit her. Dad also tried to run over Virginia with his car when she was only about fifteen. Some neighbors intervened, and he went to bed and to sleep. I can also remember the time that Dad, while drunk, ran over a person with his car and hurt them real bad. My grandparents had enough money to buy them off so Daddy did not get charged.

I was fearful most of my life. I think it is due to the fact that I had to retreat inside myself to survive. It is hard to believe now, but in those days I was very shy, passive, withdrawn, had no self-esteem, and lived in a fantasy world.

I lost my virginity to my first love who I married at sixteen years of age then moved with him to Louisville, Kentucky. My mom and little sister moved with us. We all lived in a thirty-five-by-eight mobile home. During the eleven years we were married, we had three children, two boys and a girl. We moved frequently during our marriage. It ended in 1972 when I left him. Mom still lived with us—telling me everything to do, what I didn't do right. I felt totally under her control. I felt I had to leave this situation, and I took my kids and moved to Lexington where I was able to get a job—and most of the time held more than one job.

Later on, I married Sherman, my second husband. We were married twenty years and had two more children, Kathryn Victoria and Robert Maxwell. When my husband was only fifty-eight-years-old, he died of lung cancer. I buried him with $964 I got from a cancer policy that a good friend had talked me into taking out. We had no life insurance, no savings, no house, and approximately $350,000 in medical bills. I was forty-six-years-old and still had a nine-year-old daughter and fifteen-year-old son at home. I did not even have my GED. I was working in Lexington at the Springs Motel in the morning, and at night at the Harley Hotel so we could survive. At one point I was working three jobs. One was working on a beautiful horse farm that provided a house for us. The owners I worked for were dysfunctional, and it seemed like I was moving from one bad situation to another. I only stayed there a year, then moved us to a house in Lexington, and once again found jobs in hotels.

Around this time, my son, Max, left for San Diego, and I never expected to see him alive again, but after a few years he returned home. He was filled with so much anger. When he was five-years-old, he watched his dad molest my older daughter, Rhonda. It is so sad that children have to go through this kind of life, and I have to take a portion of the blame. I should have known. I kept working all these hours and jobs. I never suspected my husband of abusing my daughter because he raped me every night when I got home from work no matter how tired I was. He accused me of being out with another man and then told me he would show me what it was like to be humiliated. I feel I failed as a mom because I did not protect my children from harm. By this time in our lives, my husband, who was a smart man, but was also lazy, cruel, and manipulative, would do no hard work. Rather than go on public assistance, I worked so I could take my children to the doctor or dentist, and have food and clothing. During the twenty-one years we were married, we owned several businesses. He had great ideas, and they could have worked for him if he had been willing to work another job to help with the bills. But he spent all his mother's inheritance on these businesses, and nothing was left for us when he was diagnosed with, and later died of, lung cancer.

After my husband died, I realized that the time had come for me to get my GED. There was an English teacher, Joyce Gash, at the Mayor's Training Center in Lexington who saw something in me I did not see myself. I was close to finishing my GED when she recommended I go to the NOSW. I applied and got a call accepting me. When Jane called, I promised her I would finish my GED since I only lacked two points on the math test to finish.

My mom told me that I should not leave Kathryn for three weeks because I had not done anything right in my life so far. My mom never sees the glass half-full; it is always half-empty. She told me I did not own a house and did not have any money, so what in the world would this school do for me? In my mother's mind, if you don't own things and have money, then you are not worth anything. I cried many tears trying to decide if I was doing the right thing by coming to the NOSW. Looking back, I am glad that I did. It changed my life and my children's lives, especially the two younger ones, forever.

When I came to the NOSW in summer 1992, I thought I was the only one who had such a terrible background; however, after our three weeks I realized that all the women had a story and that we had come together to support one another through the NOSW. It was wonderful to know that I wasn't alone anymore. For the first time in my life, I was appreciated for being myself and not a sex object for men to abuse, and for others to tell me how useless I was.

I grew up ashamed of my heritage in the Appalachian mountains of North Carolina, and up until I went to the NOSW, I had never known that there was anything to be proud of. To be taught at the NOSW about the strength of Appalachian women in the mountains was such a joy for me. All my life I had been taught and shown it was the men who were the strong ones. However, the more I learned about Appalachian women, the more I realized that I had been taught the wrong thing. I have learned that so many individuals in Appalachia have achieved many great things in their lives without a degree in higher education. When I attended the University of Kentucky, I took all the Appalachian Studies courses. I realized that many people had achieved great humanitarian status without higher education. Of course, building self-esteem goes along with leadership development, and the NOSW provided them both during the three-week intensive course. Sometimes, we forget to dream because the life we have is so unbearable that we give up.

The cultural activities we did at the NOSW were the icing on the cake for me, especially trips within the Appalachian region.

When I left the NOSW in June 1992 and went back to Lexington, my young daughter and I were homeless. I was fortunate enough to find a social worker who helped me find a place to live. I had to file bankruptcy and lost all the material things I had. As I stood in front of the judge, crying over having to file bankruptcy, he said to me, "Ms. Lakes, everything will be all right." But for me, it was devastating. Again, my mom let me know that I had never done anything correctly in my whole life.

The NOSW validated me as a person, finally, at the age of forty-seven. I went back home after the session, and a beautiful lady from one of the Catholic churches allowed me to come to her home, three times a week, where she tutored me in math. She had so much patience, perhaps because she had eleven children of her own. This time, when I went back to take my math test again, they allowed me to take a calculator in the room. I passed the test by two points this time! When Jane had asked me if I would finish my math test on the GED, and I had said *yes*, I meant it with all my heart. My word was the only thing I had left. I wasn't about to let her down!

I had yearned and longed for education all my life, and for the first time, I knew I was capable of getting the education that had been denied to me for so long. I enrolled in the University of Kentucky college of social work and received my bachelor's in social work in 1999 and my master's degree in social work in 2004. I thought that getting an education would make people like me more. What I did not realize was that I was a good person with or without the degrees. The NOSW was with me throughout my college career by guiding me and with scholarships. My youngest daughter and I were in college at the same time when I was in my master's program. I was a proud mom—I felt I was doing something right.

The self-esteem classes at NOSW were my lifesaver. The classes forced me to look at my decision-making and come to terms with being co-dependent on men. I did not realize it but my mom had in some ways made me co-dependent on her. She wanted to control my life, and she had done a pretty good job of controlling me for many years. What it did was make me vulnerable for others to take advantage of me, because I did not have a voice or a backbone to stand up for myself.

Currently, I subcontract for Big Sandy Development Area, within the Kentucky Regional Works Program. I teach job readiness activities classes in the Appalachian region of Kentucky. I love it because it allows me to give back to the young people what was given to me through the NOSW. I also work part-time for the NOSW, which I also am enjoying.

I am proud of myself now and am no longer ashamed of my life and the way I grew up. It has made me the strong person I am today. Without the intervention of the NOSW, I am not sure where I would be today. The NOSW gave me the inspiration to better my life and hold my head high!

## MARY

*"A lesson for me is wherever I go, in whatever situation I am, if I keep thinking positive with hope and do not stop praying, I am not alone."*

—**Mary**

I was born into a big family of thirteen children. I am number eight. I was born two years after Vietnam declared independence (reunification) in 1975. I am proud of having grown up in the beautiful highland mountains in the city of Buon Ma Thuot-Dak Lak province, from which I carry all my childhood memories with my family and saw the consequences of a country after the war.

Before 1975, my father worked in the Southern army, which was under the support of America. My mother had a grocery stand in the market with my grandmother. They were a beautiful couple and had a wonderful marriage and family. Our lives were happy, but people's lives began to change when the Communists from North Vietnam attacked and took over South Vietnam.

My hometown was the first city attacked. The Northern army targeted the civil house shooting and firing without letting up. This happened with no warning. Everyone ran out of their homes. My family ran and hoped not to be killed. Roads were blocked and dead bodies were everywhere. My parents had to hide under the ground in caves in the forest. After being without food or water all this time, my parents came back to their house and found Communist people occupying it. Every paper had been destroyed. They lost everything they owned—home, furniture, clothes—nothing was left.

In 1982 - 83, the new government launched the "new economic zone program." It punished people on a "black list," those who had worked with the Southern Army or for American forces. They called America *the enemy*. We were exiled into the tropical forest. We walked many kilometers on a rough road until arriving at our new location that had no name. We were in the midst of an unexplored wilderness. We made a tent and slept on the ground, hearing all the wild animals around us. During the rainy season, mosquitoes caused a lot of people to die from yellow fever. We did not have food, medicines, electricity. We had to dig the roots of whatever plants we knew of and eat them for meals.

There was much famine. Currency changed in monetary value. Inflation was extremely high. New money had less value than the prior one. Immigrants from the Northern region rushed to the South with nothing in hand. They were hungry, poor, and had all kinds of diseases.

My father was put in a "retransform center"—jail—just because he used to work for American forces. My family did not know when he would be released or if we would ever see him again. Many men never did return and were not heard from again.

The government changed the schoolbooks, and we had to learn the new Communist terms, new history. The government controlled everything. To go to school, one had to pay a lot of money and all kinds of fees.

Finally, my father was released. He came home with scars and wounds. He looked like a skeleton. It was hard for him to accept that things had changed so much under the new regime. He decided to have a little pig-breeding farm, and planted coffee and fruit trees. He also started to drink heavily.

My mother got up at four in the morning every day and walked to the market, ten kilometers back and forth. With the money she made standing on her feet selling vegetables, she brought home rice, food, and money for our school.

School started at seven a.m. I had to get up at five or earlier to review lessons, then walk seven or eight kilometers to school. I would often take a short-cut through rice fields with water up to my thighs, then cut through sugarcane fields and cross people's houses with dogs that barked and ran after me. It was a challenge to make sure I appeared in front of the class without my clothes being wet and muddy.

My family was poor, but I was still so lucky to have a chance to go to school. My mom always told us: "Dad and I don't have money to give you, but we will work hard to give you knowledge. Only education can take you out of poverty."

Watching my parents struggle and sacrifice everything to make sure their children would go to school made my heart tear inside and I appreciate my parents so much. I loved school and wanted to learn. I was thirsty for knowledge. I dreamed that one day I could do everything to see that my parents could have the good life they deserved and everyone could taste freedom and have human rights.

Unfortunately, my mom passed away from cancer when she was fifty-one-years-old. Seven years later, my father passed away at sixty-four. After Mom died, I finished school, came back to my hometown, and got a good job. My mom was my motivation and helped me to go through so much in my life.

I tried to find a way to continue my education. I went to France and French Guyana. I was there for two years in the convent Dominicaines de Notre Dame du Tres Saint Rosaire in France. Then I traveled to America to visit my sister's family and by God's will, I met a man who fell in love with me and did not want me to go back to France. He asked to marry me and I said, "Yes." My husband and I have different cultures, languages, lifestyles, but luckily, he loves, supports, and understands me.

We were living in the beautiful mountain community in western North Carolina that I now consider my second hometown. Everything was new for me in America. I was excited and at the same time scared when thinking about how to take control of my life, stand on my feet, and be a part of and help my community. I wanted the American Dream that was my mom's dream for her children.

One day, I saw an advertisement in the local newspaper about the New Opportunity School for Women. The words of the name were so strong, so meaningful, that I thought, "Wow, isn't this place what I am looking for?"

I applied and was accepted. After three wonderful weeks at the program, I came back home carrying so much energy and good feeling about how much is out there and that there are always a lot of opportunities. I have learned that education is a solid foundation for me to stand on my own feet. I learned that whatever you do, whoever you meet, always cover it with your love, your care, and do all with all your heart.

I am now taking a real estate class and will go back to college after my Vietnamese credits transfer. My dream is to become a dietitian or a physical therapist.

After the NOSW experience, I have more energy and am full of hope and courage. The NOSW helped me walk in life with more confidence. I feel so blessed and appreciate everything the school did for me and for hundreds of other women in the Appalachian mountains.

A lesson for me is wherever I go, in whatever situation I am, if I keep thinking positive with hope and do not stop praying, I am not alone. There are many generous people who want to reach out and help me and others. Like the wonderful people at the NOSW.

## SHIRLEY

*"I still return from time to time to the land that I call home, to the hills that own my heart, and to the mountains that hold a love that only a girl from Buffalo, Kentucky, can feel and know. My love of Appalachia will never go away for it runs deep in my blood."*

**—Shirley**

Twenty-four years ago, I took a leap of faith and applied for a program that I knew very little about, one that would take me away from home for three weeks, away from my children and my very ill mother. There was something about the program that had an appeal to me, something that I could connect to, yet I had not met anyone connected to the New Opportunity School. Even though the past twenty-four years with the New Opportunity School for Women has often been filled with challenges, I have had many opportunities that I would never have had without the school. I have been blessed to have met and made friends with so many people associated with the school. I cannot say how proud that I am to have an inspirational woman as Jane Stephenson to lead and guide me throughout my career.

My father died when I was two, and being the youngest of seven children, it didn't take long to realize there wasn't going to be a lot of attention. My father was a farmer and raised nearly all the food that we ate. My mother canned berries, apples, and vegetables from our garden, and made apple butter, picked wild greens. My brothers would "hole-up" potatoes to keep them from freezing. (This meant they would dig a large hole in the ground and put straw on the bottom, layer the potatoes harvested from the garden, and then put the soil back on top. Using this procedure kept us in potatoes all winter long.)

After the death of my father, my mother and brothers had to take on additional chores, so I clung to my grandmother who was always there for me. I remember her sitting in her rocking chair, smoking her pipe and, it seems, always "nussin'" a child. I don't remember my mother or my grandmother complaining about anything, and Lord knows there was plenty to complain about.

I can still remember my mother washing our clothes from water we had carried from the creek. She would hang them on the clothesline to dry, even in the wintertime they were still hung outside. Since they often had ice in them, she stood them by the potbellied stove to thaw out. She would make her own starch and iron every piece so that we were always presentable at the little one-room school we attended. We each had chores to do. Mine was to carry in the wood to make a fire in the kitchen stove my mother cooked on. I really didn't mind because I would sit behind the stove where it was cozy and warm, and read my book while smelling supper cooking. When bedtime came, the potbellied stove would be fired up and the rollaway beds would come down. I would crawl in behind my grandmother and sleep through the night with not a care in the world. I would lie in bed and watch the twinkle from the fire on the ceiling. I would awaken to the smell of breakfast cooking. I don't ever remember eating breakfast that didn't have homemade biscuits, eggs, homegrown jelly or jam, and gravy. Depending on the time of the year, we would have bacon or ham.

The winter of 1963, I was twelve-years-old when my grandmother became ill. I can still remember my uncle coming for her in his sled pulled by a mule. Not any chair was good for her so he secured her well-worn rocking chair to the sled and he and my brothers gently carried her from our house to the sled. My two brothers sat on the floor of the sled to steady the rocking chair. I still remember standing by the window thinking, "Where was she going with her Sunday headscarf on and overcoat?" She looked so funny to me riding down the creek bed in her good coat and head scarf, sitting straight up in her rocking chair. Little did I know that would be the last time I would see my precious grandmother. She died a few days later. It was in late January, and there was a big snow and below freezing temperatures when they brought her home in this big four-wheel drive hearse.

Being there were only three rooms in the house, it was a terrible situation. We had family come from everywhere because she had several children, and then there were cousins. Our neighbors moved the furniture out onto the porch. They cooked and brought food and tried to console us. I wanted none of it. I wanted my Ma back. I don't remember much about the next few days. I do remember returning to school and looking out the window and seeing the cemetery just up the hill, and thinking my grandmother was still looking out for me.

My brothers started leaving home one by one to find jobs up North in the factories. My oldest brother, who had taken on the role of father figure to the younger ones, joined the military where he would make a career. By the time I was fourteen, we had all left the land that had been in my mother's family for over a hundred years. When I graduated high school it was just my mother and me. She still raised a garden and canned, but she also did odd jobs for our neighbors to make extra money. I had gone through high school without running water, a phone, or TV. I am not sure how my mother did it, but in many ways she made sure I was a typical teenager. I had dates, went to ballgames, proms, and stayed overnight with my friends.

I married soon after graduating high school and left this world behind, or so I thought. I became a modern housewife and stay-at-home mom, raising three wonderful sons. We had a three-story brick home; my children attended private schools and I was in the PTA and the Junior Women's Club. I was able to purchase my mother a small home with a garden and do extra things for her. We traveled extensively, once going to Venezuela.

After my divorce, attempts at landing a job failed for I had not gone beyond high school and had never worked. I found myself sliding backward toward my childhood, an uncomfortable feeling, and then I heard about the NOSW.

# Changing Lives in Appalachia

In 1988, I was in the second graduating class of the NOSW. By 1999, I had completed a bachelor's degree and a master's of social work. I also achieved a certification as an alcohol and drug counselor while working a full-time job. I now work for the University of Kentucky as a targeted assessment specialist. I work in a field where I can recognize instantly when a woman can benefit from the NOSW. After all, I have been there. I have seen progress in social issues, but I also still see poverty. I still work with women who are victims of domestic violence. I see families torn apart by drug addiction and families reunited. I still see a lot of love.

I have twenty-four years of wonderful memories with the NOSW. There have been many milestones since I attended. I have experienced births, deaths, graduations, and new jobs. I have witnessed changes in the school leadership and in my personal life. I have traveled from Chicago to New York City on behalf of the school. I have been to the *Oprah Winfrey Show* and had lunch in Trump Towers. I have referred twenty-six wonderful women to the school and have watched as their lives have prospered—just as mine did.

I still return from time to time to the land that I call home, to the hills that own my heart, and to the mountains that hold a love that only a girl from Buffalo, Kentucky, can feel and know. My love of Appalachia will never go away for it runs deep in my blood.

## SADIE

*"I hope to set an example and instill the desire for education to as many people as possible. I want to be an asset in helping to break the cycle of drug and alcohol abuse, mental illness, and violence. This is my unbridled dream for my family, community, and mankind."*

—**Sadie**

Life takes many twists and turns, and sometimes we're left at a crossroads, wondering where to go next. It's hard enough when we're young and just beginning to find our way, but even more difficult when we are mature adults and suddenly realize the need to start over. As a young adult, I never thought I would need anything more than a high school education. As life's difficulties approached with age and maturity, I realized the wisdom I thought I had was really just foolishness. The school of "hard knocks, cuts and bruises" made me see the need to start over. I recognized the need to create a new and better life for myself, but was uncertain where to begin.

I was born and raised in a very abusive, alcoholic, dysfunctional Marine Corps family, a middle child of six, the first to receive a high school diploma. Vowing never to live the life I was born into, I was determined to "rise above" the alcoholism, mental illness, and domestic violence. My mother struggled for many years to protect and nurture her precious children. It was her only reason to keep breathing. The strength, love, and tenderness she tried to express were not appreciated until after her death.

The man I fell in love with and married had a drug and alcohol problem. For years I endured a volatile relationship. My life centered on him. We were always going to dope parties, shooting cocaine, drinking, and smoking pot for days. He worked construction, which gave me the chance to travel some. The downside was that he always had his crew living together with us. I was the "old lady of the house" who had the job of cooking, cleaning, and washing for all the guys.

When he finally stopped loving me, I was so devastated I just wanted to die. I became so depressed, I don't remember what happened for several days—only that I stayed curled up in the recliner and kept telling myself to keep breathing. Neighbors and friends checked in on me, but I couldn't do anything. I lost ten pounds in one week.

Somewhere during this time I decided I needed to protect myself and had a neighbor go with me to buy a shotgun. I was afraid of weapons and guns, but now, was more afraid of him. My depression turned into alcoholism. At times I had suicidal thoughts, seeing blood splattered over the walls. I was having a breakdown and finally went to the doctor.

Throughout my husband's unfaithfulness, drug addiction, beatings, and incarceration, I had stayed with him. Now, I was a middle-aged divorced woman. I found myself at loose ends, wondering how to survive the rest of my life. I had acquired a good deal of hard, practical work skills, but I was exhausted physically and emotionally. Yet I always had a burning zeal to help others improve their social circumstances.

But the first key to helping others was to help myself.

I decided to take advantage of the free services offered at the local adult education center. With no previous exposure to a computer, my quest for knowledge kept me focused to keep striving for additional education. I found myself searching out more free programs that were vital in my passion for further education.

A longtime librarian friend kept bugging me about this NOSW program in Berea so I decided to send off for an application. I filled it out and was accepted. A new revelation as to the opportunities and educational prospects available to me began to unfold.

At the NOSW, I learned and shared with others. We were all there in the same shoes but wore different colors. I learned to first love and take care of me, instead of everyone else. I learned how to quit living in the past and focus on the future. I came to appreciate the Appalachian heritage that was similar to the southern plantation culture of my grandparents in South Carolina. I was so doggone proud and excited about the things I was being infused with, I could hardly wait to get home and get busy.

I set for myself the goal of an AAS degree in human services from a local community college, which I earned in 2008 with high distinction. I believe human services addresses the real needs of our basic society and is the heart and soul of our existence. It means a selfless giving of our time, strength, compassion, and resources to educate, encourage, and persuade. There is a tremendous demand in social services concerning drug abuse and the prison system. I want to be instrumental in helping slow down the revolving door of the prison system. This is my passion and mission of "paying it forward" to help break the cycle of violence and develop a new collaborative approach of positive reinforcement for further generations.

While going to college, I worked and volunteered at the adult education center. I mentored the newer students. I then got a part-time job as an instructional assistant, then became a substitute teacher's aide, part-time, for the school system.

I was alive and on fire with enthusiasm. I was applying for scholarships and winning some. Finally, I got a full-time job with the local community action center. Wow! I had benefits, insurance, retirement, and paid vacation. I am currently working there but feel the pressures of a nonprofit organization with limited block grants and budget cuts.

I decided to try to reach out even more. I applied to the local library, since they had just completed new construction. I was hired part-time as a circulation clerk one night per week and every other Saturday. The library is the central station for this county. There is always something to do to help patrons. With grant money, new computers were bought. The only catch was that classes had to be taught on them, so can you imagine how I felt when I was asked to teach about online resumes and job-search skills? I reflect on my first resume that Stephanie Beard, the career counselor at the NOSW, helped me to create. She made me look so good on paper by learning from me what my skills were. I enjoy helping my class do the same.

I have lived and seen the results of alcoholism, domestic violence, and abuse. I have seen the struggle and sacrifices that my mother made to provide and protect her children. During my childhood, there was no public assistance with food or housing. There were no abuse shelters or counseling. Yet these problems and issues remain today. It is this way of life I wish to help prevent. This is the gut-wrenching strength and sacrifice that my mother instilled in her children. My mother's sacrifice, along with my faith and belief in Jehovah God, the creator of mankind and His written Word, the Bible, and my focus on His son, Jesus Christ, have given me the privilege to work for our families and neighbors to help them and others.

The NOSW provided me with the tools and the desire to continue my education. I learned Appalachian culture is a vital one worth being preserved and appreciated. The classes and opportunities to make pottery, jewelry, and a collage helped me express my feelings and place my life experiences in those designs. I currently display them in my office as a reminder of the struggles I went through. I use them as a teaching display for clients who need direction and advice.

I hope to set an example and instill the desire for education to as many people as possible. I want to be an asset in helping to break the cycle of drug and alcohol abuse, mental illness, and violence. This is my unbridled dream for my family, community, and mankind.

# Part II
# THE PROGRAM

*The mission of the New Opportunity School for Women is to improve the educational, financial, and personal circumstances of low-income, middle-aged women in the south central Appalachian region.*

## THE WOMEN OF THE NEW OPPORTUNITY SCHOOL

It is Sunday evening and opening night of a three-week residential session of the New Opportunity School for Women in Berea, Kentucky. Fourteen women have arrived from all over central Appalachia to spend three weeks living in a residence hall on the Berea College campus. The women have left home, community, and family, most with great fear and apprehension. All the way to Berea, many thought they should turn around and go home. It is not unusual for a participant to sit in her car for an hour or so while "getting up the nerve" to come inside and face the unknown. All are uneasy in this new setting, but all are determined to change their lives.

Upon their arrival in early afternoon, a New Opportunity School staff member meets each woman, and helps her get settled into her room and meet other participants. A new arrival from a distant county, CJ, remembers:

> *The day the New Opportunity School began, I was so nervous, but the folks helped me relax within moments with their kindness. They listened to each story and provided support, and we felt an emotional spirit that they had for each person there. We were all feeling grief from all the trauma we had gone through, and we knew this was a time we needed to be able to get rid of that grief. I was treated like a person. I have never had such wonderful treatment, and during the three weeks I really began to feel like a real person and not a useable object.*

It is seven p.m., and after a good meal at a local restaurant, the time for group sharing begins. The women sit in a circle along with staff members as they listen to the history of the program. Soon the emphasis is on the participant. Each woman talks about why she has come to the NOSW, what she expects to take home from the program, and any of her personal history she wishes to share.

Thus it begins. Boxes of Kleenex are passed around. The stories of child abuse, domestic abuse, alcohol and drug abuse are told again and again. Through tears, we wonder: Why do our Appalachian women still live lives of poverty and abuse? Why are they still dropping out of school, getting married, and having children at such an early age? Why can't we prevent these lives of bare existence, hardship, living in cars, shelters, or substandard housing? How can we help these women with little or no educational opportunities and the low self-esteem that comes from little money, no health care, constant physical and emotional pain and suffering, and being put down by society, family, and often social service agencies designed to help them?

These and other problems were recognized at least fifty years ago when Presidents John F. Kennedy and Lyndon B. Johnson, declared the War on Poverty, focusing on the Appalachian region. The Appalachian Regional Commission (ARC) began in 1965 as a federal agency to address the persistent poverty and growing economic despair of the region, which includes part or all of thirteen states. (See appendix for list of states.) There is no doubt that through the years, the ARC has contributed to economic development, more educational opportunities, easier access to the mountain region, and funding for better access to health care. (For more information, visit their Web site at arc.gov.)

During the 1960s, many media outlets produced sensational stories about Appalachia. The stereotyping continued and multiplied across the nation and the world. As a result, Volunteers In Service To America (VISTA) volunteers arrived, as well as many other well-intended "outsiders," who, although they knew almost nothing about Appalachia, hoped to help the region's people improve their quality of life.

Greta, a graduate of the NOSW, wrote in an unpublished essay of her first encounter with a VISTA volunteer:

*When the VISTA workers came in the 1960s, that was about*

the time I was in the eighth grade and they came to our house. They were doing all this poverty work. At first, Daddy was real suspicious. He didn't see any way they was going to help us—that the only thing that we were was some sort of curiosity. I still wanted to believe that there was hope for things to get better, because there really was not any kind of work and nothing to look forward to as far as ever having more than we had.

I remember the first two VISTA workers that come to our house was this girl from Pennsylvania and a boy from California. They come together and Daddy invited them in and they talked about where they were from. The way they explained it was that they were in school, and this was sort of like a school project and they had come to live in our county for a certain period of time. They wanted to get to know everybody. I remember the boy talking to Daddy. He didn't say we was doing anything wrong, but the toilet was built up over a creek that run down by the house and the creek was usually dry. It was out far away from the house and it sort of stood on legs. Well, when it would come a rain, it would flush it. So the boy said, "Why don't we dig a hole and build a new toilet because, you know, flies and that kind of thing gets into the poopy and they'll carry it into the house and onto the food." He just kind of reasoned with Daddy so they ended up changing it. They helped us to dig a hole and build a new toilet. They became friends with us. The girl ended up marrying a boy from the head of the holler. She was not a good judge of character—he was worthless and had quit school when he was seven. I think he got work in the mines right before they got married, but it didn't last long. He drunk a lot and was real abusive to her. I think she only stayed about six months. She had a baby and she took her baby and left, and nobody ever heard anything else from her.

Yet for decades, despite new programs and opportunities, very little changed in the lives of local women. They dropped out of school, married early, had several children by age eighteen, lived with a husband who couldn't settle into a job, then suffered years of struggle and abuse with poor health, and no education. Living day to day defined their life situations.

According to 2010 census data, roughly half of female-headed families with children were poor in Mississippi (51.2 percent), Alabama (49.2 percent), West Virginia (48.7 percent), and Kentucky (48.5 percent.) All these states include counties designated Appalachia.

Today, the educational gap is higher in Appalachia than other parts of the United States, and the gap appears to be growing. According to data from the Appalachian Regional Commission (using census data from 2006 – 10), in southern Appalachia only 22.8 percent of the adult population over age twenty-five have graduated from college. In every Appalachian state except New York and Pennsylvania, Appalachian counties have higher proportions of all populations *without* a high school diploma and GED. Fifteen percent of the population in the United States over age twenty-five have less than a high school diploma, but the percentage in Appalachia Kentucky is 28.2, the highest of any Appalachian state.

For twenty-five years in Berea and eight years in North Carolina, the NOSW has been combatting these problems and improving lives of Appalachian women. Seventy-five percent of the women who have graduated from the NOSW have become employed, are in school for further education, or both. Almost 700 women, with an average age of forty-two, have completed the three-week intensive residential program. Eighty percent of the participants have family incomes of less than $10,000 a year, and many less than that. More than half are single parents, and those with husbands often support the family because the husbands are disabled, ill, refuse to work or, at best, can't find a job.

The mission of the New Opportunity School for Women is to improve the educational, financial, and personal circumstances of low-income, middle-aged women in the Appalachian region. The focus is on Kentucky at the Berea school and on North Carolina at the program at Lees-McRae College in Banner Elk, North Carolina. By May 2013, the NOSW expects to open a new program at Bluefield College on the Virginia and West Virginia border.

The program is free for participants, including funding child care back home, transportation to the program site, room and board, and any other costs associated with the three-week-session.

An important feature is that the women leave their home and community environment for three weeks and completely concentrate upon themselves—a luxury most have never had. While at the NOSW they envision an improved life for themselves and learn how to turn their dreams into realities. They learn that the NOSW staff truly cares about each woman and wants her to succeed. No matter what poor choices they have made in the past, all are equally loved and supported. They have a clean slate upon arrival as no one but the NOSW staff knows their past. The women feel they have been given back their self-respect. CJ describes her feelings:

> *During my times in court, I was introduced to a safe house where I could go and talk about anything that was on my mind. During one meeting, I met a lady who talked about her experience coming to the New Opportunity School, and I did some research and learned more about the program. I thought I was so much older than the others would be, but I wanted to try the program. I knew I needed more help to get over the stress I had endured for years. But I also felt I was not good enough or smart enough to go to this school. But I applied and was accepted, and little did they know that just through the opportunity to go to school that I had been enlightened by being accepted. This was the beginning!*

# THE PROGRAM

Although they may be greatly disadvantaged by past and present life circumstances, the women have a strong desire and high motivation to change their lives. They are intelligent and hard-working, but they have had few opportunities, and little encouragement to seek a better life.

The early life of the participant plays a significant role in determining her future. CJ writes:

> *My story begins when I was born into poverty. I didn't know, growing up, that we were poor. Only when school began and I didn't have clothes and shoes like the other children did I understand.*
>
> *At six years of age, I was sexually molested by a family member. During those times, no one ever talked about any situation that went on in the family. I lived in fear of what was going to happen. The only good outcome was that the rest of the girls in our family were protected against that family member.*
>
> *I felt no one wanted to be around me because I was unclean and not good enough. I have always felt my body was a window and everyone could see inside. I knew I could never trust anyone again and that my childhood was taken away. As I matured, insecurity set in, and I was unable to be sure of myself. I was told: "If you don't talk about it, it ain't there."*

Sue shares her early years growing up in Letcher County, Kentucky:

> *I was the youngest of six. We lived in a small town where my father was a coal miner. I was abused at the age of eleven by a family member. My father passed away when I was fourteen, and by that age I was married and had a child and another one*

> on the way. My husband was abusive but he was good to the kids. Things were going downhill, and by the age of eighteen I had three children. I had no education, no car, so I had to stay with him. Eventually, I left him when my children were twelve, eleven, and five. Then he took the kids away from me. He knew the judge in the county, so I lost custody of my children. I never got to see my children after that until thirty years later.

After several months in a shelter for women, Sue met her third husband and, with his support, started GED classes that led her to the NOSW. She has reconnected with her children, enjoys her grandchildren, and works as a property manager in charge of twenty-nine units.

Family struggles occur for many reasons. Karen writes about her young life:

> I come from a strong family of workers and people who have had to struggle all their lives. My father was faced with learning he had leukemia and that he was dying and that he wouldn't even live to see not one of his kids grow up to be eighteen-years-old or see any of his grandchildren to come. I was nine-years-old when my father was faced with making a decision of letting us stay with our mother or sending us to a children's home in Pine Ridge, Kentucky, called Dessie Scott. He chose the latter because he knew my mom wasn't able to give all eight of us kids the attention and care that we needed and deserved. My dad had family issues dating back to when he was a child, and I am sure that was a factor when he made his decision to put us in the home. I'm glad he did because it gave us stability and structure. I also came to know about God while at the home due to going to church, and one of my fondest memories is getting baptized while there. I know and believe it was my dad's dying legacy that we be taken care of when he separated from this

*Earth. I am so proud of my father. I only hope someday I can make him as proud of me as I am of him. My mom is a really strong person also. She endured a lot of pain from us being taken away, but she has a lot of inner strength, and I admire that in her. I wouldn't trade my family for no one in the world, and even though we had rough times, it's those times that we actually pulled together to have a strong family bond.*

Unfortunately, not all families have strong bonds and caring parents. A constant theme that runs through the lives of a large number of participants is the role alcohol has played in their lives. Any money the family might have went for the purchase of "spirits," often creating a situation where the breadwinner in the family was too incapacitated to hold down a job.

George Ann describes her family situation growing up in the mountains of North Carolina:

*The first glimpse of life for me was that of fear. My dad instilled fear in my mom and the kids to try and keep us around. My dad was an alcoholic who did not know how or what to do with his problem of alcoholism, other than to take it out on the ones who were closest to him, which was my mom, me, baby sister, and my older sister who fought for all of us even though she was a child herself. (Dad could quote the Bible with the best of them and thought he was called to preach the Gospel but never did.) I can remember all of us sleeping in the woods, and Dad kicked over the stove in the house, and we watched it go up in flames and smoke, believing that Daddy was in there; however, he wasn't. During the fire, I remember crying about Grandma's churn and a green dress that a neighbor had given me which Mom would not let me wear unless we went to church. I can still see and feel that green taffeta dress as if were yesterday.*

> *For some reason, on holidays Dad made sure that he was drunk. We were having supper, and a neighbor was eating with us, and Daddy got mad at him and was cutting the man's shirt off with a hunting knife, but the man got mad at Daddy and pulled a gun and held it to Daddy's head and told him to go lay down. I can remember crawling under the table so that I did not have to watch. I can only remember putting up one Christmas tree, and Daddy got drunk and knocked it down. We never received gifts, and we never gave any gifts. One time, a neighbor made their children share one thing with us. We never celebrated birthdays either—we were just glad that we made it to another day.*

Time after time, the women in the NOSW talk about how they were made to feel inadequate both at home and at school. Teachers played a large role in how these young girls felt about themselves. Some teachers were cruel and responsible for girls dropping out of school. On the other hand, one woman in the NOSW confided how a teacher in her elementary school befriended her, told her how smart she was, gave her clothes, and ultimately the courage to stay in school. Unfortunately, when she left for middle school elsewhere, she no longer had a teacher-friend to encourage her and got no encouragement from her alcoholic parents. She dropped out in eighth grade, got married at thirteen, and had five children by twenty-one.

George Ann expresses her strong feelings of inadequacy as a young school girl and describes her treatment by her teachers:

> *I grew up knowing and believing that I was inadequate in every aspect of my life. No one ever said to me, "You are smart and can do anything you want in life." I can only remember the first grade of school and Ms. Buchanan whipping me in front of the whole class for having bubble gum in my mouth, telling me how she was disappointed in me for not following*

*the rules. Another teacher used to lay me across her wheelchair every morning and spank me in front of the whole class because I did not have my math homework done. I remember telling my dad that I was not going back to school, and he went and talked with her and she never spanked me again. I would love to know what he told her. However, the damage was already done. I thought I was a worthless child and no one believed in me. There was also a teacher who had me stand in front of the blackboard all day long trying to do a math problem, which I could not do, and then my cousin sneaked up behind me and told me the answer. Can you imagine the humiliation that a young person of my age suffered at the hands of someone who was in authority?*

*I grew up being shown that I was a "second-hand person" due to being a woman. My mom still feels like that and still holds men in a higher regard than she does women.*

Despite her bad experiences in her early schooling, George Ann always yearned for more education. After attending the NOSW, she enrolled in the University of Kentucky and completed a bachelor's degree and then later a master's degree in social work, which she proudly received at age sixty-one. Interestingly, George Ann also relates positive things in her past such as never going hungry as they put out two gardens each year and a whole field of corn. Her daddy killed a hog on Thanksgiving Day and a calf every fall. She grew up without an indoor bathroom and remembers a plank across the creek to the outhouse. They carried wood and water every day to their house, and her mother washed clothes on an old wringer washer. Not having TV, the children in the family roamed the mountains, and even though she left home at age sixteen, she still loves her mountains and longs to be back there. Yet, she knows that most likely she will never live there again.

Many of the NOSW participants grew up in a loving home, but negative external influences and low self-esteem consumed and dictated their lives in ways that are often hard to understand. One young participant, Erin, writes in her life-story of her early use of alcohol and drugs beginning her downward spiral into the world of addiction. Even with a loving, supportive family, through boyfriends, marriages, and the births of two children, the addiction continued. Today, Erin is drug-free and finishing her last year of college.

Health issues in childhood also play a strong role in the loss of self-esteem. Children can be cruel by teasing, bullying, and ignoring each other. Rose writes that she was three-months-old when she had her first seizure.

> *My grandfather ran with me in his arms to meet my parents so they could take me to the hospital. The doctors told my parents that I would not live past the age of five, and that if I did, I would be severely mentally retarded. My mother refused to accept this and said no. She was right, and the doctors were wrong.*

Rose took medication for years which enabled her to attend school. However, she continued to have seizures in school and was ridiculed by other children.

> *I was the stupid, diseased child that was avoided and mocked by others. In fact, I was not stupid. I couldn't read because I needed glasses, something that was not discovered until I was in the fourth grade.*

Rose completed a bachelor's degree and a master's in psychology and is currently searching for a job in her field.

Participants often talk about childhood illnesses, such as

rheumatic fever, that kept them behind in school. Eventually, not being able to catch up with classmates and friends, they dropped out. Many young Appalachian girls are not encouraged to continue school but rather to get married and have children. Many get married early to escape their family situation, only to find themselves trapped in an even more difficult life. CJ married young and describes the disintegration of her marriage:

*In 2008, the bottom dropped out. My life came to a halt. There in our home, words began to fly back and forth until anger set in. He came at me with a flagpole, pushing me against the wall, yelling in my face "You don't talk to me like that." I was in fear for my life. He had acted with rage before to scare everyone, and I didn't know what was going to happen. I knew I was not going to let him beat or hit me. I mustered up enough strength and guts to place my hands on the flagpole, and I pushed with all my might. He landed against the wall behind him. His fists were at my face, and he was yelling and threatening to knock me to the floor.*

*I backed away and headed toward the bedroom toward his bedside stand. I could hear him behind me. I reached into his bedside stand and pulled a gun out, pointed it toward him and said, "Get away from me." I then pointed the gun toward the floor. He stood there in complete surprise, saying, "I'm going to take a warrant out on you." He turned his back and walked out the door.*

*The following day was a nightmare. I was arrested. After that I was homeless for a while. Without my children, I don't know where I would be today. They always knew how their dad was. I thank God for the babies He gave me. They have stood beside me through all my trials.*

*Everything was taken from me. All money was removed from our checking account, my car insurance canceled, my health insurance canceled. I was put out of my house. My job was gone because of the charges I had against me. This was his control—take away everything and I will crawl home.*

*I went through courts for the next two years, and finally the charges were dropped, and all charges were expunged. I thank God for this. I am so thankful for family that stood by me. You know, so many folks are put into your path at any given time and we may not know why. As I look back over my life and can see clearly, I know how blessed my life has been.*

Divorce, abandonment, and widowhood are other factors that prompt women to seek help from the New Opportunity School for Women. However, there are also cases where strong family ties and supportive husbands exist, but emotional distress precipitates the need for a woman to seek help. Such was the case for Lillian:

*I was in my forties, holding down a factory job, and caring for my two children, and my husband was doing part-time and seasonal work. My world was somewhat normal. Then the rug got pulled out from under me.*

*My mother was diagnosed with Stage Four lymphoma cancer. She was my rock, and I felt she was the only one I could turn to when things went wrong. She lost her fight for life in February 1995. Then in October 1997, my son Ricky was on his way to work on a rainy Sunday morning when he lost control of his car, and I lost my son. I think that this is really what put me over the edge.*

*My next few years were spent in a fog-like state. I would get up and go to work, come home and sleep. It's a wonder that my daughter has turned out as wonderfully as she has.*

*Then I found an article about the NOSW in the local paper. With the encouragement of my daughter and my husband, I applied and was accepted to the next session. This turned out to be a new beginning for me and my family. Even after graduation from the program, it took awhile for the lessons to really sink in, but slowly and step by step I began to make small changes that have changed my world. My husband and I took out a loan and bought a house. Then I applied for and got an office position at a factory. I began to volunteer for the New Opportunity School in their clothing closet. This was a way for me to give back to the organization that gave so much to me.*

The reasons for attending the NOSW are as varied as the lives of the women seeking help. They come searching for a better life and brighter future especially for themselves and their children. Many times a women comes because of encouragement from children who say, "Go for it, Mom." Marilyn is a Kentucky native who had moved with her parents to Ohio when she was four-years-old. She relates her return to Kentucky as an adult to be closer to her parents who, after many years, had returned to their old home place:

*I had worked in Ohio, but I really had no skills to help me find a job. While checking the newspaper, I saw the ad for the NOSW. I showed it to my oldest son who was living with us at the time. Without telling me, he wrote school staff and told them why they should consider me for the program. When I received the letter accepting me, I was overjoyed.*

However in other cases, mothers of participants often do not encourage their daughters to break away from their current lives to go to the New Opportunity School. Some have been known to threaten them if they venture into this unknown world. They make comments such as, "You are getting above your raising," or "You can't make it there—you will just get sent home in disgrace." It takes extraordinary courage and determination for the daughter to break away.

On the other hand, many of the women have had an especially close relationship with their mothers and want to care for an ailing parent. Charlene had very little confidence after a failed marriage that left her devoted to the care of a young son:

*When my son was five-years-old I met Frank, the man that I am married to now. He took my son into his heart and life as though he was his natural father. After many years, I found my way back to my mother who was remarried. Frank, my son, and I began spending more and more time with my mother and stepfather. It was great for a long time. It seemed like overnight that my mother became ill. I came to the rescue again. I believed that I was supposed to take care of everybody. I began making all the trips to Mom's to take her to the doctor and hospital, and I was still working all the time. That Thanksgiving was a horrible time for me. My mom was in the hospital with a heart attack and my husband had to have his arteries cleaned out. Then two years later, my husband fell off his truck at work and badly damaged his shoulder, neck, and back. He could not go back to work after that. I began working two jobs, then three, to keep the bills paid. I did that for nine years.*

It was several more years before Charlene could find her way back to caring for herself.

Family members left back home sometimes fear participants will change and fear how it will affect them. Perhaps the women won't return home, or perhaps they will be different and want to make changes in the family structure. These women have been the rock of the family and without them, what might happen to everyone else? It is true that the women may return home changed and with determination to have better lives for their families. However, they rarely return home wanting to abandon them.

It is important to understand as much as possible about the family circumstances of the participants to help women learn how to make changes within the family structure. A few years ago, when a NOSW staff member called to tell Betty she had been accepted to the NOSW, Betty was thrilled. She began excitedly talking about her arrival time, and asking questions. But in the background, her husband could be heard saying, "You are not going to go. You are *not* going to go." Another male voice, her son, was heard saying, "Aw, Dad, let her go, let her go." In further conversation, we learned that Betty's husband was diabetic. She gave him daily shots, prepared his meals, and constantly looked after him as well as their teenage children. The NOSW paid for a person to come in daily to give the shots and cook meals, and Betty was able to attend the NOSW. After she graduated and returned home, her husband realized that she was not going to leave him, and he became a big fan of the program. Both were volunteers for several years.

A life-altering event such as a serious accident or the death of a spouse can dramatically change the life of a woman who had previously been leading a comfortable life. Marilyn Daneen, an energetic woman from North Carolina, relates:

> *After a series of unfortunate events, we were in a serious car accident. I wasn't able to work for at least six months, and my husband's neck was broken and he needed many surgeries. We were not able to keep our phone and could not pay the power bill or rent. I became very depressed, and my health and state of mind were heading for a breakdown. Having a*

> *thirteen-year-old daughter with no support coming from her father caused me to cry when she wasn't looking. I felt like I was a terrible mother and a worthless dependent person. My marriage crashed. My daughter and I had nowhere to go except to the local shelter. There, I met a person who had great passion for her work, and she saw something in me that led her to encourage me to attend the NOSW. My life has changed in so many ways since being in the NOSW. Once hopeless and now confident, I have become a strong, motivated single mom. I am now a very happy person!*

We cannot know all the reasons or obstacles that keep women from taking advantage of opportunities for self-improvement. Hundreds of women in our region never find the inner strength to make the life-altering decision to attend the New Opportunity School for Women.

Many hear about the program and the time is just not right to make the decision to come. Yet for most who do attend the NOSW, it has not been an easy decision. Jean, an older woman with great determination, tells about making the decision to apply and later attend the program:

> *I had torn the announcement out of the newspaper and stuck it on the wall with a straight pin by the telephone. It read: "The New Opportunity School for Women is accepting applications for women who want to better their lives." This is for me and I want to go, I thought. But it was several more years before I could fulfill this dream. Each time I reached for the telephone I looked at the paper on the wall. That paper turned from white to brown to a dark gray, the edges curled up and beginning to disintegrate, and still it hung on the wall. The straight pin was now rusty and the scrap of paper was dated 1987. Several years had passed. It was 1999. That dream kept me going.*

*Many times I wondered if I would ever get a chance to do something for me.*

When a woman does find the courage to attend the NOSW, she most often has a life-changing experience. Chrissy, a recent graduate, said:

*I went from a sixteen-year-old dropout to a forty-six-year-old grandmother of eight and college student. It's all because of my three weeks at NOSW and all the support around me.*

## THE THREE-WEEK EXPERIENCE

How can you change a life in three weeks?

It is hard to answer that question because one has to understand the program's total integration of the educational, cultural, experiential learning, and the careful mentoring of individual participants by staff, instructors, internship supervisors, and key volunteers.

**Classes in Literature and Writing**

The first class on Monday morning is Appalachian Literature. Before coming, the women have received four books to read. Books are carefully selected to introduce participants to strong Appalachian women they can identify with. Wilma Dykeman's *The Tall Woman* is set in the period of the Civil War and highlights a woman holding her family together during trying times. In Gwyn Hyman Rubio's *Icy Sparks*, a young girl overcomes disabilities that are not understood by her family and neighbors. In *Kinfolks*, Gurney Norman's book of short stories, relationships between family members, a strong grandmother, and other strong female characters echo relationships held by participants in their own lives. A varied selection of poetry is also required reading. *Courageous Paths*, a book of nonfiction stories of nine NOSW graduates, helps readers understand the NOSW as they embark upon this adventure themselves.

Although many of the women are not readers, mostly because they were not introduced to interesting books and writers while in school, they get excited about the books they read for the Appalachian Literature class. Discussion is lively and nonthreatening as each person's opinion is respected.

The structure of the Appalachian Literature class is much like that of a college class, giving a window into what they might expect if they should decide to seek further education. Through the years, we have been asked how teaching Appalachian Literature helps the participants get jobs or encourages them toward more education and training. It is our experience that Appalachian women who are low in self-confidence value themselves more after learning of the region's wealth of well-known writers. After taking the classes, women will strive to write, to express themselves, and to seek even more knowledge for themselves and their family members.

Creative writing classes, taught for twenty-five years by Kentucky writer and poet laureate, Gurney Norman, open new doors as participants learn they, too, can write. They are led through writing exercises that encourage self-expression. At the NOSW program at Lees-McRae College in Banner Elk, North Carolina, Professor Michael Joslin teaches creative writing much as he teaches his college classes, while also putting together a book of the participants' best writings for them to take home.

Gurney Norman has been a member of the teaching faculty of the New Opportunity School for Women in Berea since its founding. When asked recently to write (specifically for this publication) about how he teaches this class, Gurney wrote the following, which is an excerpt from a longer essay entitled "If You Can Talk You Can Write."

> "At ten a.m. on a Thursday, usually in the second week of the three week NOSW session, we sit around a large, oval-shaped oak table, a dozen NOSW women and myself, all of us earnestly writing by hand in journals or on regular sheets of paper. I will have begun the session by telling a brief story from my personal history, perhaps about my grandmother with whom I lived as a child. I will have explained that this grandmother was a country woman who lived on a hillside farm and worked hard to raise the food we ate and milked a cow twice a day for our milk and butter. After raising eight children of her own in this basic, old-time way, my grandmother took in three grandchildren, my sister and brother and me, to care for throughout the World War Two years and for some years

beyond. I describe her long work days which began at four a.m. when she fixed breakfast for my grandfather before he left to go work in the coal mine.

"I usually take about five minutes to tell this personal story. After my description, I ask the women sitting around the table to think of someone in their early lives who cared for them and describe them.

"For the next fifteen or twenty minutes, the only sound in the room is that of pens or pencils scratching words onto paper. The women are taught computer skills at the New Opportunity School but I want us to write by hand because of the tactile nature of such writing. Hand writing is physical, real, immediate. It is also an ancient practice that, in my opinion, is connected to our processes of thinking, remembering, dreaming. Most of us will write two or three pages in twenty minutes. When we have finished writing, I invite the class members to share a portion of their new writing by reading aloud. The emphasis is on the word 'invite.' There is no requirement to read aloud. Actually there are no requirement or demands at all in this approach to writing. We are not in formal 'school' with its rules and requirements. The premise is that we are in a safe, relaxed environment where individual adults are free to participate in the proceedings at any level they are comfortable with.

"The newly written personal and family stories are often very moving, sometimes funny, and always articulate and honestly expressed. Often one person's story reminds others of their own similar stories, and for a while there are animated exchanges across the oak table. Soon enough, though, I move us on to the next writing exercise by telling another personal story. Sometimes I hold out my left hand and point to a scar in the flesh at the base of my little finger, then tell the story of how I got the scar.

"When I was in first grade, on the way home from school one snowy day, we boys started throwing snowballs. I scooped up some snow that had a piece of broken glass in it, and it cut my hand. I remember how deeply red the blood was against the white snow. For some reason I held my hand out and watched the blood fall into the snow as I turned myself around, dripping blood in a circle.

"'What are the stories behind your scars?' I ask. 'Including emotional scars.'

"Soon everyone has two or three or four pages of new writing.

"This time, instead of reading aloud to the whole group, I have everyone get a partner and scatter around the room and take turns reading their new words to each other, knowing that animated conversations and more stories are sure to come as a result.

"With about fifteen minutes left in the morning session, we return to the table where I take a few minutes to make a few general observations.

"Clearly we all have much to write about. Most of us know so much more than we realize. Writing is a way to see into our own minds and to organize our thinking, which can be a source of personal power. We have all had times when our lives have been chaotic and our memories are fragmented

# Changing Lives in Appalachia

Gurney Norman, who has taught creative writing for the New Opportunity School every year since 1987, is presented an NOSW shirt by a participant.

and jumbled. There is something truly satisfying about finding the words that put a shape to our rambling thinking, and getting those words on paper. Once we get even a brief version of our remembered experiences down, we can develop it, add more words and expand the stories, a process which can be its own kind of pleasure. And of course writing down our stories is a way of preserving them for the children and grandchildren in future years. Except for letters, no one in my family made a record of the family history, but I remember with great fondness the many times as a kid listening to the older people talk about the past, about colorful relatives and significant events two generations before mine. I was lucky in that I inherited family lore through an oral tradition. To have a sense of one's family history, even if the stories are painful, can be a source of comfort and stability as we take power over them through writing.

"Then we adjourn. The next morning we meet again around the big table and continue our work. We only have two sessions together, usually a Thursday and Friday, two hours each time. It isn't much but I am always impressed by how much we do accomplish in four hours. The natural language of the women who come to the New Opportunity School is beautiful and their stories are beautiful, too, as they put the truth of their lives on paper.

"No one learns more in our writing sessions than me. I learn all over again about my family background, the difficulty of it and also the richness and the greatness of the mountain people I grew up among. The women of NOSW feel like family to me, like sisters and aunts and nieces, all of us bonded by the lives we have led and the stories we share with each other. I think everyone associated with the School is inspired anew by the spirit and courage of the women who attend. Each time I attend a function of the School I am reminded of its uniqueness, its purity of purpose, its excellence as an organization, the righteousness of its effect on the women who attend and also on the many good people who in their different ways support the work of the School."

What a unique opportunity the participants experience by having this wonderful man devoted to the NOSW and the women who listen to his words of encouragement to express themselves in writing. From Gurney's encouraging classes and writing exercises spring a love of writing that the women remember long after they return home.

Participants tell us it is impossible to explain to family and friends the pride and self-confidence they feel when their ideas, written and oral, are validated in these and other classes.

Charlene describes her own writing experiences after attending the NOSW:

*I am currently taking writing courses. I have two short stories almost ready to send to a publisher, I am starting my own greeting card company, and the choir director at my church is working hard to put music to one of my poems titled "Celebrate." I will soon be giving a class at church, "Healing Through Writing."*

Encouragement from instructors leads many graduates to continue their education in English, creative writing, or journalism. Bobbie tells her story of returning home and enrolling in a local community college:

*During a job fair at Roane State, the coordinator introduced me to a reporter from the local newspaper. They were looking*

THE PROGRAM

*for a part-time reporter. Was I interested? Was I ever! He told me to see his editor the next day. I went and the editor hired me then and there. This was like my dream come true. Although I was making only six dollars an hour, that was more money than I had ever made in my life. I felt this was what I was born to do. My first book of poetry,* **Appalachian Heartsongs,** *was published by Publish America in 2008. However, since they don't promote their books, it has sold very little. I have many more poems and have written my autobiography. I would like my next published work to be by a publisher who will try to promote it.*

Alma is also enthusiastic about her classes:

*Then there was Appalachian Literature and the Creative Writing Class! I learned that I had a gift to write about the Appalachian that is inside of me. I wrote a poem that won third place and was published in a book called* **Spoon River Anthology.** *The poem was called "A Panther" and was about the time when I was a very small child I saw a panther on a log. I still love to write stories and poems.*

What a great boost of confidence to know that your poems and articles are being read and enjoyed by others. Combined with other classes, especially classes in self-esteem, in three weeks NOSW participants enjoy successes that give them confidence for trying new things in the future.

## The Power of Self-Esteem

But true change cannot occur without a change in identity. This shift occurs only when participants learn how to value themselves.

Following the Monday morning Appalachian Literature class, the first of four self-esteem classes is offered. It has been taught for twelve years by Janie Polk and, more recently, assisted by Bobbie Burcham. Materials were developed especially for the NOSW by these two exceptional instructors who know and understand the participants' need for building confidence and trust in themselves.

Janie Polk, long-time instructor of the self-esteem classes, writes: "My job is to teach the women to believe that they are worthy, loved, okay, and in fact, special. This counters all they have been told about themselves by husbands or various family or community members who tell them they are nothing, unworthy, and losers. Most of the participants are aware of their lack of self-confidence and how it has held them back through their lives although they may not be able to express this concept."

The book, *Feel the Fear and Do It Anyway*, by Susan Jeffers, serves as the main text for the class. Janie Polk believes that "fear is a mainstay in most lives, and though it can help keep us safe if carried too far it becomes our greatest obstacle in life." She believes the participants must recognize and understand fear if they are to develop fully.

All class sessions are treated with confidentiality as participants share painful life stories, including ones of abuse, that have damaged any confidence they may have had at some point in their lives.

Many stories are heartbreaking. Audrey, a forty-one-year-old widow describes where she was in her life before coming to the NOSW and how the program helped her focus on a future of which she had never dreamed:

> *I live in a very small town in Eastern Kentucky. I have been a widow for nearly three years. I have a background of twenty-one years of severe domestic violence that ended when my younger brother killed my husband during a big fight. My brother had his throat cut and my husband was beat to death. One year later I went to the NOSW, and they let me know I have meaning in my life. They showed me the courage and*

*intelligence that was really inside me. I had lost all my self-confidence and thought my life was over. NOSW let me know quickly that I can have a life. I had never had anyone care for me before NOSW. They even helped me get my teeth checked and cleaned. Even if I am from Appalachia, I am somebody. I am starting college and going into the legal field to help domestic-violence victims. Thanks to NOSW, I have the confidence and support I need to go to school.*

Early childhood experiences contribute heavily to lack of confidence, as well as the poverty experienced by the women growing up.

Charlene writes:

*There were three of us children at home. I had a sister who seemed to be perfect in every way. She was neat and tidy—not me. She got straight A's in school—not me. She quickly became the favorite. She could do no wrong. I became tired of being asked: "Charlene, why can't you be like your sister?" At first I thought I was only imagining the favoritism that was going on, until my girlfriend asked me why my parents seemed to not want me around as much as my brother and sister. This was a total blow to what little bit of self-confidence I had. Naturally, I began to cry and my friend apologized and hugged me. I think that was the day that I withdrew from the real world. I began living a life in a fantasy land. I hardly stayed at home and went to my friend's house as much as I could.*

*My self-esteem was always low, and my parents did not understand what they were doing to my self-confidence when they continually compared me to my sister. I grew up thinking that everyone was better than me. In my imaginary life, I was* very special. I could do things that no one else could. I suppose that I hid away for most of my life, even after becoming an adult.

When Charlene was seventeen she met a man who joined the Marines, then sent for her to come to Hawaii to be married. She was certain her dreams had come true, and now she could leave home and live as she pleased. Charlene continues:

*Everything was great until I got pregnant with my son. Then Lee decided that he did not want to be married anymore. What little bit of self-confidence I had built up was destroyed with one sentence: "Charlene, I do not love you anymore; I want a divorce." My life was a complete shambles until I had my son. After he was born, I built my entire life around him. I was determined to provide a good home for him. I became very good at my job and was making good money, finding another hole to crawl into. I became a workaholic. I was happy, or so I thought, as long as I could provide for my son. There was no time for anything for me—after all, I didn't matter anyway. My son was the most precious part of my life. I ate, slept, and breathed for him for the next thirty years. I kept putting myself on the back burner, having no idea what I was doing to myself.*

Attending the NOSW was life-changing for Charlene, especially the self-esteem classes:

*The classes were all valuable and important. I could never express in words all the important things I learned there. The self-esteem instructors were such important factors in me finally finding "the real Charlene." I had begun to think that Charlene was dead and buried, as I had not seen her for such a long time. My fellow "sisters" and I began to open up and share some of our worst secrets with one another and our instructors. How wonderful it was to be able to say anything about our lives and not be judged. We laughed together, cried together, and were always there for each other.*

Self-esteem is changed and bolstered by learning new tools and strategies, and learning that beliefs, even long-held ones, can change. As the first class progresses, Janie passes out rubber bands, asking the women to wear them on their wrists. Janie then tells the women that every time they speak negatively about themselves, they are to "snap" themselves. She explains, "This gets them used to listening and hearing themselves express how they feel about themselves. They begin to consider why they feel that way. They begin to ask, where did that message come from? Thus begins the awakening of the thought process, and introspective conversations are initiated."

Exploring the power of making positive decisions, Janie observes, "The women do not know they have the right to ask for what they want, to change their minds, to say no, to make mistakes, and to speak up. In other words, their voices have been stymied and effectively silenced."

During the last week of the program, Janie and Bobbie lead discussions about how we resist change, how threatening it is, even when desirable. They try to fortify the women for what's ahead—what they will face when they go home. They help the women understand how they change as they grow and that something that sounded or seemed perfect as a teen, may not be true now as an adult. Janie maintains the building of self-esteem is a life-long process. She explains, "We are taught to not judge but are never given the tools to help us understand how to do it. Comparison is a personal way to judge ourselves and we must learn to appreciate what we have, who we are, and only look at others for ideas and ideals. Forgiveness must eventually come, but boundaries and standards

(I will not be hit!) are ours to establish through education and learning. Compassion, the feeling for others, is essential."

Another exercise developed by Janie is to encourage the women to understand their rights: the right to say no, to ask for what they want, to make mistakes, to be allowed to say "I don't know," and to change their minds. Janie brings articles from home, such as placemats, dishes, scarves, jewelry, and other interesting gifts and places them on a table in front of the participants. She tells the women they can have almost any of the articles, but that they have to ask her for them. She also tells them that there are articles that she will not give away so they can expect rejection. At first, the women are hesitant to ask, but the fun begins and they begin asking en masse. Janie also leads discussion on when it may not be appropriate to ask for something they want while also giving the women a "voice" so they no longer feel timid or afraid.

The women speak highly of this class in their evaluations, and many continue to correspond with Janie for years as she continues to counsel them long-distance. One participant wrote Janie that,

> The greatest thing that I have experienced through the NOSW is that I don't have to go through life beating up on myself or letting other people do it to me. I have learned to be an advocate for myself.

Of the women who have been in her classes through the years, Janie says: "I have never encountered rudeness, inattention, or any negative feedback as the women love this subject. They desperately want to learn and are so very, very willing to study, work hard, or do whatever I ask. Year after year, the women are so wonderful—smart, loving, possessing humor, and hunger so for education. One can't help but love them, as well as being horrified at what they have endured!"

In the eight hours of class, Janie and Bobbie cover numerous topics. Participants are given many handouts as it is impossible to absorb all the information given in such a short time. The women often tell us they read and study these materials after they go home and highly value their notebooks.

Offering self-esteem classes early in the three-week session allows the women a taste of what they will experience in the days to come and encourages them to stay with the program. Staff and fellow participants always encourage and give special attention to any women showing signs of leaving the program for any reason. Very few have returned home before completing the program. Experiencing the caring staff and instructors is a major feature of the success of the New Opportunity School. A trained, licensed counselor is also on staff during the three-week session. Office hours are announced and appointments are scheduled at the request of the participants. The counselor is also on-call for emergency situations.

Beginning as a component of the self-esteem curriculum at the NOSW at Lees-McRae College and recently included at Berea is a class in Expressive Arts. It is designed to empower participants and increase their sense of competency through the Story Quilt experience, to help the women explore their own personal stories, and to create a shared story in the form of a quilt. Doing so creates a visual record of their unique contributions to NOSW and serves as a gift to the school and future participants. Participants are asked to visualize an image representative of their own personal story. It can be an image of the transformation they are undergoing at NOSW, something they want to let go of or hold on to, an image of their true self, or a particular story that represents each individual. Completed quilts are hung in the NOSW offices for all to enjoy.

"Understanding Personality Styles" is a workshop taught by Peter Hille, who is trained in administering and interpreting assessment tools. Through discussion, participants determine the characteristics of their personal style. This is helpful in understanding how they relate and interact with family, friends, or at work. Peter describes the workshop: "For the women of the New Opportunity School, who are engaged in a profound journey of self-transformation, this class provides another way to look at themselves and others, seeing both strengths and areas for potential growth. I have always tried to emphasize that everyone is fine just the way they are, even though they may be different from each other and different from other people in their own lives. We share laughter, sometimes tears welling up from deep reflection, and 'aha' moments of insight and self-understanding."

Because many participants have faced domestic violence, discussion is encouraged about this topic and it is referred to in many classes. "Understanding Violence Against Women" is an important class that allows the women to express how they feel about themselves when they have encountered violence in their lives and then how to work through those feelings.

**New Work, New Lives**

One of the key goals of the program is to help women become capable of entering the professional world of work, thus assuring financial independence.

Learning and/or refreshing basic skills is an essential part of the NOSW program. Classes in computer basics, punctuation, and math review give the women an opportunity to reinforce their knowledge and learn new skills. Several computer basics classes give participants knowledge of the Internet and E-mail. An account is set up with instructions for how to E-mail one another and the NOSW staff after they return home. They learn about Facebook and many stay connected to each other and NOSW through social media. Although many participants do not own computers, most have access to one through their local or county library. While those with children are more likely to have computer knowledge and access, many have never connected with or experienced any training.

Classes in job search skills are offered by our career/education counselor, Stephanie Beard. Almost immediately, the women start developing a resume. Most participants have never thought that they had enough job experience or skills to develop one but through individual conferences and conversations, the women learn how to turn their skill sets into a resume they can use when they return home and start the job search process. According to Stephanie, "It is freeing for the participants to compile the needed information about themselves on paper, see it transformed into something they can feel proud to distribute to employers, and learn they are more employable than they had expected."

Interviewing techniques, including mock interviews, help ease anxiety about the job-search process. The NOSW also has an extensive clothing closet of gently used dresses, suits, and accessories, from which the women select clothing appropriate for a job interview, with help from the clothing closet coordinator, Lillian Pratt, a graduate of the NOSW, and other staff. Makeovers include a visit to a local hair salon. An informative session on makeup by a local beauty products representative is an especially enjoyable event. After returning home and interviewing in their communities, many phone the office to share how what they learned in class gave them an advantage. The confidence they have developed from learning job-search steps is undeniable.

An important part of the NOSW program is an internship. Every afternoon participants arrive at carefully selected internship sites. Before coming to the NOSW, they have been given an interest inventory to complete and return. The inventory is professionally scored and compiled to reflect career fields parallel to their interests. From this test, as well as personal interviews with each woman, the career/education counselor selects an appropriate internship. One participant, Mary Ann, says:

> *I felt my internship was the best! I was a docent (a tour guide) for the Banner House Museum. I discovered I loved the*

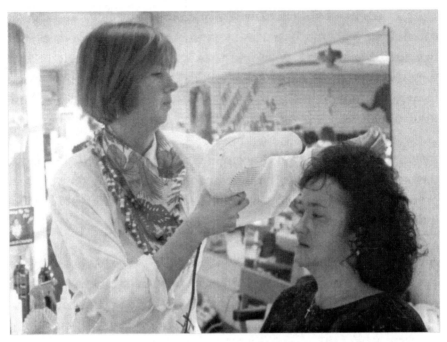

NOSW participant Linda Lamb has her hair styled during a makeover by a volunteer. The makeovers are a regular part of the job-readiness curriculum.

*historical items and I loved giving tours. The other docents treated me with respect, and we became sisters as we worked together even though our time together was relatively short. On my last day, I was given gifts and cards, and I felt as though I had made good friends.*

With three weeks of job experience through these internships, the women leave with a professional reference and with the confidence they can face the world of work. They also leave with a plan that includes what education or training is needed to complete the requirements for their chosen profession.

Throughout all the classes, participants are encouraged to think long-term. We often say, "Think career with benefits—not just get a job, any job." Of course, there are women who, because of their financial situations, must find a job immediately. However, we encourage them to think how they might turn a short-term job experience into a long-range career goal.

One graduate describes her experience after completing the program:

> *I am working part-time at (a local health care clinic) for twenty hours a week. I will soon start volunteering at the hospital where I did my internship, hoping to get hired full-time.*

Fortunately, several graduates have been successfully hired to work at their internship site, and many continue to volunteer until they have even more work experience.

Through their internships, many women learn that they need more training and/or education to enter a new career. A session entitled "Is Education in Your Future?" is led by college admissions counselors who describe all the options available through community colleges, four-year liberal arts colleges, and state universities. Admissions requirements, application procedures, and financial aid options are explained. Women are so inspired by the possibility that they really can go back to school, many immediately apply to higher education institutions and are in school by the following semester.

Many women at the Berea program want to attend Berea College because no tuition is charged; however, admissions requirements regarding test scores are very high, and often, women who have been out of high school several years or who have taken the GED tests some years back are not readily admitted. Nonetheless, several NOSW graduates have been admitted, have graduated, and are now gainfully employed. Since the NOSW program in North Carolina is an outreach program of Lees-McRae College, and the women live on campus, they have access to campus staff who can lead them through the application procedure. One recent semester, two NOSW graduates immediately enrolled at Lees-McRae and are now successfully completing coursework with high marks. The college faculty, staff, and administration feel "ownership" of the NOSW program and its graduates and help in every possible way to assure a successful college experience. Often, we hear from Lees-McRae College President Barry Buxton about how he had breakfast or stopped on the sidewalk to talk with a NOSW graduate and college enrollee. He reports how proud he is of their accomplishments. This kind of support by college employees is experienced over and over during and after the session, and the women gratefully respond with even more enthusiasm for this giant step they are taking into their futures.

Even if participants are not ready to take the leap into further education for themselves, they are gathering information and knowledge for their children and grandchildren, especially by learning about financial aid. Before, college had never seemed to be an option. But living on a college campus for three weeks and listening to college staff explain admissions requirements has led to a large number of NOSW family members obtaining college degrees. One NOSW graduate, Teresa, upon enrolling and doing well at Berea College, encouraged her husband to enroll. Later their son enrolled at Berea College, and now all three are proud college graduates. Another graduate, Sharon, writes:

> *My decision to go to college has changed not only my life but the lives of others in my family. My son is currently working toward an associate degree in automotive science. My oldest daughter is currently attending college for her associate in science, too. My youngest daughter is in ninth grade, and I am homeschooling her while I work on my bachelor's degree in agriscience education at North Carolina Agricultural and Technical State University. By graduating from the NOSW,*

*my family's educational goals have changed for the better and I am eternally grateful.*

The New Opportunity School also has education scholarships. These funds can be used not only for tuition but for books, child care, and transportation to college. During the past ten years, over $85,000 has been awarded by the NOSW in scholarships for our graduates. A dream for the future is to make the fund open to the NOSW graduates' children and grandchildren.

Another graduate, Linda, a highly regarded respiratory therapist at a large hospital in Texas, credits her internship supervisor with giving her the knowledge to enroll in a nearby school:

*After finishing the NOSW, I was accepted in respiratory therapy school. I received my certification in respiratory care, and while in school I worked at Berea Hospital. After graduation I became a full-time employee and worked there for five years. Later I moved to Texas and started work at Hendrick Medical Center, where I am still employed after eighteen years. I have received several awards and was employee of the month. I was featured in a video used to train new employees.*

Besides a fulfilling career, Linda describes her busy and productive life:

*In 2010, I also started a craft business in which I make football pillows and blankets and sell candles. I also work part-time at a rehabilitation center taking care of special needs children. I have worked in the voting polls and participated in the Relay for Life and Bunco for Breast Cancer. I am a faithful member of my church where I work hard for the Lord. My son is now thirty-six-years-old, and he is a band director in a high school. His wife is a teacher. He graduated from the University of*

> Kentucky and also has his master's and is now working on a second master's and his doctorate in educational leadership. My daughter is twenty-eight-years-old and is married and living near me in Texas.

Before attending the NOSW, Linda was folding clothes at a laundromat making two dollars per hour. After NOSW, she was able to support herself and children while going to school, and instill in them the desire for an education. She was an inspiring role-model.

Peggy, who attended the first NOSW session in 1987, remembers how she felt about her future as she went back home after graduation:

> I was offered every opportunity to attend Berea College in the fall. The staff said they would make sure I had an apartment and a job. But due to my personal life, I couldn't move to Berea. My daughter was in law school; my son didn't have gainful employment and lived with me. I was sure something would open up for me and it did. After returning home and to my old job, a longtime friend came and asked me if I was interested in a new job. Yes! The state had passed a new law that there would be a family resource center in each and every school in the state. I was given the job as assistant to the coordinator of the Whitley Middle School Family Resource Center. My salary tripled. I retired from this job in 2008 and managed a gift and flower shop my daughter had opened in downtown Whitley City. Then I worked in my daughter's law office. I have been taking classes at night at Somerset Community College.

Peggy also became very involved in her community through performing and writing for the new McCreary County Performing Arts organization. Through many traumatic times in her life she has had the courage to seek new opportunities for herself and her family.

## New Worlds: Leadership, Government, and Cultural Activities

Very few women with backgrounds of low educational achievement and from low-income families can envision themselves in leadership positions. Yet, these intelligent women have the innate skills to be leaders and advocates for themselves and others. The question then becomes: how can you convince them of their abilities? The goal is to instill in them a desire to go home to volunteer and work within a structured environment, such as a nonprofit or local school attended by their children or grandchildren.

The answer lies in the leadership component of the three-week program, a set of classes and field trips. "Developing Leadership Skills From Within" is the first class. They study a checklist of skills people in leadership positions have. They then check their own skills against this list. They conclude they, too, have the qualities to be leaders but perhaps do not know where to start. The next class, "Speak Up and Be Heard," helps women formulate what they might say in making a presentation about an issue in their children's schools, churches, or community organizations. In a basic public speaking class, women learn to feel their fears about speaking out and do it anyway in a loving, caring environment. They also learn how to serve on boards of organizations while role-playing as club officers. A copy of Robert's *Rules of Order* is given to each woman to take home.

As one graduate, Alma, writes:

> *Another class that I still use is the speech class taught by Mr. Paul Power, who told us that no matter how many speeches you give, you will have butterflies in your stomach. I have learned this many times as I've given speeches in my church, at a regional retreat, and even talked at NOSW graduations.*

In a class called, "Getting to Know Your Government," the women learn how and where to find help through state, local, and federal assistance programs. After this class, a trip to the state Capitol for the Kentucky program and to county officials in the North Carolina NOSW makes participants even more comfortable seeking this type of help when needed. At the North Carolina program, a session is held with local women who are mayors of their towns, and the women have an opportunity to think about themselves in a similar role in their futures. Over the years, several NOSW graduates have run for county office after returning home, and even if not elected, they are proud of themselves for having had the courage to face a political opponent.

Early in the NOSW program, it was learned that an astounding number of participants do not vote, many because they do not know who to vote for. During every session, the women learn why their vote is important, how to register, and the staff makes a plea to them to make that be the first change in their lives after going home. A recent survey indicated that 87 percent had voted in the last election, a critical change in the community life of the women.

Participants are encouraged to make a difference in their own communities through volunteering when possible. One graduate, Katie, wrote:

> *I volunteer at Friends of Paint Lick two days a week. I attend the Paint Lick Christian Church on a weekly basis, and I love helping out there whenever I can. We formed a local food bank for emergency food in this area. It was formed by five churches in the Paint Lick area and I am the spokesperson for this group from our church.*

Throughout the three weeks, every effort is made for the women to participate in cultural activities, a new opportunity for most participants. Since the three-week session is on or near a college campus, many cultural events are taking place: theater performances, concerts, lectures. Field trips to museums are made available. Many women living in rural areas have not had opportunities to delight and experience these activities. Participants go home enthusiastically seeking ways to provide an opportunity for their children to experience similar events.

**Lives Improved Through a Focus on Health**

It would be unrealistic to not consider health issues of participants. Before coming to the NOSW, each woman must fill out and return a health form that lists all current and previous medical conditions, as well as current medications. Due to their low-income level, the women have had very little opportunity for preventive medical care. Dental care has been nonexistent. Some participants may have suffered from depression for years. They may have learned of the NOSW through therapeutic professionals, including those in drug and alcohol rehab facilities. (A participant must be drug or alcohol-free for a year before being accepted to the NOSW.) As the application procedure requires two letters of recommendation, it is often a drug counselor or a health professional that serves as a reference.

It was discovered in the early years of the NOSW that few participants had ever had even a baseline mammogram. Arrangements are made during each session for women to have both a mammogram and a Pap smear at no cost. Results are mailed to their doctors or a health department. Unfortunately, twenty-five graduates of the NOSW have died. Early detection could have prevented many of those deaths.

Poor dental health affects the overall quality of health of a participant. Many women have had teeth pulled as the only alternative available to be rid of a toothache. Some women lack upper or lower teeth, or have gaps that need partial plates. Fortunately, a generous foundation has awarded funds to both NOSW locations for a dental fund that graduates can apply to for dentures or partial plates. Besides improving health, having new teeth builds self-confidence.

Because the participants of the NOSW come to us from a variety of life situations, such as shelters or rehab programs, on occasion the staff must work with an individual to find housing after graduation and determine, "Where do I go from here?" We emphasize throughout the three-week program that once they graduate from the NOSW, they are with us for life! For many, this is an unusual concept. Many have been through programs they have been "put in," and when that program ends, there is no further contact with the agency. Graduates from the NOSW know they can call any staff member at any time for advice. They receive newsletters, attend reunions yearly, and are invited to regional alumni chapter meetings. Every two years they receive, complete, and return a survey so we know where they are and what they are doing. Now that many women have access to a computer, E-mails are often sent by staff reminding women of scholarship deadlines, workshops in their areas, and general information about the NOSW. Keeping in touch with our graduates is time-consuming for the staff but critical to the success of the program and our graduates.

**With Graduation Comes Rebirth**

After a successful three weeks, day and night instruction, successfully learning to live with other women, heads chock full of new learnings, graduation day is here! Family, friends, and donors are invited to the graduation celebration and banquet, usually held at Boone Tavern Hotel in Berea, or at MacDonald Dining Hall at the Lees-McRae College program. The event is always well attended, with 125 to 150 people arriving to celebrate the NOSW graduates. The women are expected to introduce themselves and talk briefly about how the program has helped them and what their future plans are. Graduation certificates are awarded and each woman receives a small gift. Graduation attire comes from the clothing closet, and with their new makeovers, the women look wonderful and are so proud of their accomplishments. Graduates from previous years are invited and asked to speak if they wish to do so. It is a joyous occasion of love, accomplishment, gratitude, and sharing with family, friends,

THE PROGRAM

NOSW Founder and Director Jane Stephenson and her husband, Berea College President John Stephenson, congratulate a graduate in 1989.

and donors. For the staff, it is another rewarding end of a session of changing lives of Appalachian women.

A caring, hard-working staff is crucial for success. Our dedicated staff works long hours during the session and never complains. They are always enthusiastic and helpful, listening to any problems, driving vans to events, attending classes and programs with the women, and always being on call and present. The "house sister" staff position is filled by a graduate of the program and lives in the residence hall with the women. For many years, Mary Absher, a graduate of the Lees-McRae NOSW, has been house-sister at both programs. Mary has an excellent rapport with the women and an understanding of their needs. Volunteers are used in various ways, including leading class discussions, helping with the clothing closet and makeup sessions, preparing food, and generally supporting participants.

**Into the Future**

Important to the success of any nonprofit is the board of directors. Engaged board members and a strong committee structure play an active role in ensuring the organization continues to operate efficiently while paying close attention to its mission. Strategic planning, financial stability, and active fundraising and friend-raising make for an organization that runs smoothly and efficiently. Although the board of directors at NOSW at Berea is a decision-making board, a NOSW branch that is part of a college campus' outreach efforts will administratively answer to college officials but may have an advisory board that is a support organization for the program and staff.

A good fundraising plan and having adequate staff working with a volunteer board is necessary to ensure the continuation of any nonprofit. Proof of the need for a program such as the NOSW is essential, as are evaluations that prove the program's viability and success. The New Opportunity School has been fortunate and is grateful that financial support from dedicated donors, foundations, corporations, church and civic groups almost completely funds the NOSW in both locations. There are always times in the life of a nonprofit when you wonder if you will make it financially. A catastrophe, such as a recent fire that destroyed the Berea NOSW office, may happen. The spirit of an organization must be one that is willing to work hard and get beyond problems that will, inevitably, arise.

There is no doubt that without all the many, many extraordinary people who have worked tirelessly these twenty-five years, and the nearly 700 courageous women who have had the fortitude to stick with and graduate from the program, this miracle program would not have succeeded.

The New Opportunity School for Women will continue to be an important source of guidance and inspiration for the next twenty-five years. Not only will the two locations that now exist continue, but new programs in other states will begin. Changing lives of Appalachian women for the betterment of the women and their families will always be our goal. These courageous women will continue to be our inspiration.

## THE RESULTS

Over the years, constant evaluation of the NOSW program has been key to its success. Participant evaluations of the three-week session include not only classes, internships, events, and facilities, but also staff, instructors, and supervisors. Evaluation tools are constantly changed, updated, and evaluated. Any negative criticism is taken seriously with changes made in personnel, location, and approach to the topic and any other part of the program not meeting our stringent requirements.

Many times we are asked, "How do you know your program is changing lives?"

The answer: Because our graduates tell us. Every two years since the NOSW's inception in 1987, graduates receive a survey in which they are asked what they are currently doing, how the NOSW has changed their lives, if they are employed, and other pertinent questions.

Results from the most recent survey (2010) tell us:

- Although 75 percent of our graduates were receiving public assistance while attending NOSW, when answering the survey, only 28 percent were still receiving this type of assistance.
- When asked if their financial circumstances had improved since graduating from the NOSW, 73 percent answered "yes."
- Additionally, 87 percent indicated their personal circumstances had improved since graduating from the NOSW.
- When asked if employment circumstances had improved since graduating from the NOSW, 67 percent answered "yes." From the survey we learned that 56 percent were currently employed full-time, part-time, and/or self-employed. (Many graduates from the early years of the program who were employed have retired. However, the survey did not ask specific questions regarding retirement, so it is unknown how many of those unemployed

were actually retired.) Of those who were unemployed, 14 percent were unemployed by choice and 57 percent because health issues prevent employment. Eleven percent were unemployed because they were enrolled in an educational institution. A great benefit to becoming employed is having benefits, especially health insurance. It was gratifying to learn that currently 71 percent now participate in a health insurance plan.

- When asked the type of degree, certification, or training the graduates had completed, 80 percent have completed a master's, a bachelor's, a two-year associate degree and/or a certification program. Another 20 percent had also completed non-academic coursework for self-improvement.
- Early in the program in our leadership classes, we learned that very few women voted and an unusually large number were not even registered. Added to our leadership curriculum was a section on the importance of voting. Interestingly, from the most recent survey we learned that 89 percent are now registered to vote, and 79 percent voted in the last election.
- Volunteerism is also encouraged. During the program, participants are asked to consider the problems in their own communities and how they might work toward positive change. The recent survey indicates that 65 percent of the respondents are currently volunteering in their communities.

The recent survey offered graduates an opportunity to comment on how the NOSW had helped them in the past, how the staff continues to be of service, and what they might need in the future.

A 1998 graduate wrote:

*I am grateful for my NOSW experience. I was afraid of going out on my own, but NOSW gave me the courage to try to change my life. My husband has become ill with heart trouble so I have taken on more work. I cannot tell you how important the computer classes are. Now I know how to get on the Internet and I see how much one can learn. This old dog is learning new tricks!*

A graduate of the 2006 program wrote:

*The NOSW has been invaluable to me. The love, support, and the more tangible qualities (such as scholarships, clothing, etc.) that I received and continue to receive have enriched my life beyond measure. I have a lot of health problems currently, but I intend to return to school, get a degree, and contribute to NOSW and the world in general. I attribute to the NOSW my desire to help others. I wasn't always so altruistic. Thanks.*

A graduate of the 2009 session wrote:

*This is such a worthy, life-changing experience, not only for the person attending, but in the way it continues on down the line through other family members even though they were not there. The NOSW will probably affect our future generations! Now that is powerful!*

Sometimes, our graduates express problems they are having, and at the same time, the hope they feel for the future. For example, one graduate wrote:

*Life is very hard, but I know that I can get through. I am going to school and working now, and life has become really busy. But I feel a lot better about myself, and I know that I am on the right track to a better life. Thank you all for your encouragement.*

As one woman explained:

*To me the NOSW was a chance of a lifetime. I wish every woman could attend. I feel more alive now. I feel like myself again. Before the school, I had got so depressed because I felt like my life was over because I couldn't work. Now I feel like I may be able to work again with the education that I am now getting. I also felt before coming to the NOSW that I was too old to go to college and begin again. Now I know that I'm not. I see a future in my life again.*

Another graduate focuses on the opportunities the program presented to her:

*I really enjoyed attending the NOSW. I got to take part and do so many things that I never got to do before or since. I feel my outlook is much greater. My expectations are higher. I don't feel so limited. I realize and see the choices and opportunities I never saw or knew before or even thought were possible to achieve. My quality of life has improved. Thanks so much for all you do and offer to other women like me.*

A graduate of the 2008 session wrote:

*The NOSW has given me a sense of security within myself that I have never felt before. I feel empowered. I have been truly blessed to attend the NOSW. No matter where I go in life, I have gained insight within myself, and for the first time in my life I realize that I am important to myself.*

The importance of building good self-esteem is reflected in the words of one graduate:

> *All of my life I wanted to be somebody and to be normal like other people. When I finished the NOSW program, when I walked I didn't look down at the ground. I held my head a little higher. I told myself, I guess I am as close to being somebody as I will ever be. Thank you!*

Of course, as in any program that spans twenty-five years, there are women who are lost to us. Some moved and left no address, twenty-five died, and there are graduates whose contact is intermittent. So much depends upon how their lives are progressing toward their goals and how much continued help they need from us.

We will continue surveys every two years, always evaluating our effectiveness in helping Appalachian women and their families achieve more satisfying and productive lives.

A member of the first NOSW class of 1987, Carolyn Phillips, from Beattyville, Kentucky, studies for class. (© David Stephenson)

# Part III
# TWENTY-FIVE YEARS of HISTORY

## IN THE BEGINNING...

Can a phone call change your life? How about two phone calls? How many lives can be forever changed?

That's how the New Opportunity School for Women began and how lives all over the Appalachian region have been changed! You have read the stories of some of the lives of the brave graduates of the NOSW. Now you will learn how it all began with a phone call from my friend, Gurney Norman.

Gurney wanted to know if Berea College, where my husband was president, had a program that could help a female friend learn self-confidence, how to get a job, and improve her financial condition. She was experiencing an unexpected divorce and would soon have to support herself and two children. She had no skills, no education, and very low self-confidence and didn't know where to turn for help. Berea College had always been at the forefront in outreach programs and in 1925 began an Opportunity School during the month of January where adults would come to campus, live in a dorm, and learn whatever they wished to learn—usually on a one-on-one basis with a faculty member at the college. Based on the Danish Folk School tradition, these adults spent evenings folk dancing, getting acquainted, and making decisions about the rest of their lives. I once met a man whose life work had been repairing radios—a skill he learned at Berea's one-month Opportunity School. Many of the young adults attending the school went on to become full-time students at Berea College. The school operated for twenty-five years until 1950 when the enrollment had become so low that the administration made a decision that there was no longer a need for such a program.

At this time, it was 1986. Gurney's call prompted me to talk with my husband about the dire straits of many rural women, especially in the Appalachian region and most especially in the eastern Kentucky area in which we lived. The women I had concerns about were low-income, under-educated, and many were living lives filled with abuse, poor health, and with a sense of hopelessness. How could Berea College help these women?

My husband, John Stephenson, a very caring man and a dedicated Appalachian scholar, knew exactly what I was thinking and felt it fit well with the mission of the college, but a program of this type could be very expensive. Women we would want to help by bringing them to Berea for such a program couldn't pay the cost for attending. Where was the college to get these funds?

The second life-changing phone call was received by John a few days later from a foundation that had made a previous grant to Berea College for an innovative and successful program. Their question to John was: Is Berea College considering any other new and different programs that needed funding? John immediately thought of our discussion regarding Appalachian women and said to the program officer, "Would you be interested in a program to help low-income, under-educated Appalachian women become more financially secure, find jobs, and become better educated?" They responded positively and indicated the proposal deadline—five days away.

John phoned me from his office to tell me the news and suggested I get busy writing a proposal. Many years before, I had attended a workshop on proposal writing but never tried writing one and had actually forgotten most of what I learned. I knew I needed help.

I got on the phone to call together as many people on campus I could think of that could help design a program for women. The group included Sidney Farr, known for her writing about Appalachian women; Barbara Power from the college library who could give the participants a tour of the library and help structure campus internships; Diane Kerby, who managed the facilities available at the college; Anita Barker, the college counselor; Dorothy Coffey, the college career counselor who was in charge of labor positions on campus; Ruth Butwell and Gloria VanWinkle, who were in student life and had always shown an interest in the adult students who were enrolled at the college; Tom Arnold, director of the alumni office who could recommend alumni who would help us recruit and recommend women for this new opportunity; Janice Blythe, from the home economics and family studies department and manager of the home management house where we hoped to house the women; Debbie Powell, who worked with special programming on campus; and Stacia Berry from the college development office. Gurney Norman couldn't attend, but we talked many times by phone as he described his friend and what her needs were. Gurney even offered to teach creative writing to the women to help them express themselves in a positive way. We both felt it was very important to help the participants understand their own culture and feel a sense of pride of place.

An atmosphere of great excitement prevailed at that first meeting in the living room of the president's home on the Berea College campus. What a productive brainstorming meeting that was! Ideas flowed. Debates took place. Would the program be for a month as was the old Opportunity School? No, the women would want to go home for a visit at the end of two weeks and they might not come back. How about three weeks with no break? Could the three-week session be held during the summer when residence halls were available for housing for participants? What about their children? Could they bring them to campus? If so, what would they do all day? (Berea College did not have childcare facilities at this time.) Could they have jobs (called labor positions at Berea College) on campus as all students do? Could women in our region really leave home and family for our program and stay an entire three weeks? Who would teach the classes—after we decided what these classes would be? A big question was the amount of funds we would ask the Foundation to award us.

I started to write the proposal but had to stop occasionally to phone people for advice, especially Rod Bussey, vice president for development. I would stop writing to try to convince my husband to write the proposal for me because I didn't know what I was doing. Fortunately for me, he said, "No, you need to learn to do this." Of course he was right!

By the end of the week, the proposal was ready to be faxed to California and we all anxiously awaited the answer. Just before Christmas 1986, the call came to John that the Educational Foundation of America would award us $28,000 over two years. Our program would receive $14,000 a year—the amount requested.

Imagine our excitement! Now the hard work must begin to get the program ready for the summer of 1987. John suggested the name for the program—the New Opportunity School for Women, in honor of the former Opportunity School and to also let any women interested in applying know this was a new opportunity for them.

An advisory board was established, made up of those people who had gathered at my house that afternoon and had thoughtfully given good input and ideas. My own experiences working with returning adult students at the University of Kentucky, the job I held before we moved to Berea in 1984 when John accepted the presidency, were invaluable to me as well.

Leigh Jones, vice president for financial affairs, offered us an office on Main Street recently vacated by the *Berea Citizen*. I looked at surplus furniture that the college had gathered and found a desk, a table, a sofa and a couple of chairs. Tracy Grubbs, the labor student assigned to me, bought supplies at the College Book Store, and we moved into a second floor room above shops along Main Street on the college campus. After about a month in this location, it became obvious that this was not going to work as an office location. There was no convenient parking and it was hard to tell women not familiar with Berea or the college campus where we were located. Often I had very little time to work on this project during the day, and Tracy and I were not comfortable working there alone at night.

The president's home had a small bedroom on the first floor which had originally been the house manager's office when the home was built in 1932. Why not make it the official office for the New Opportunity School? My husband didn't mind, college officials thought it a good idea. The move was made and a new phone line installed for the program. Our kitchen table was used as a working space, our living room for a meeting room. It worked beautifully for many years. Often John would stop in the kitchen to help us lick stamps and give his opinion regarding brochures, schedules, and other matters.

It seemed the whole campus was thrilled about the program. The public relations department offered to write a news release to send to county newspapers in the region we would serve. Tom Arnold consulted alumni records and phoned and made appointments with alumni who were in "helping professions" in the Appalachian region, telling them about the program and asking them to help recruit. Tom and I traveled many miles that spring talking about our program with people in the region that could refer women to the NOSW. Our mailing list became extensive as people would send names and addresses of people who might want to know about this new program. Campus office staff volunteered to have participants in a labor position (currently referred to as internships).

My time was filled with figuring out a realistic budget to cover the cost of the program, the three-week schedule, and logistics of starting up such a program. We hoped to have fourteen participants, two of whom would be selected from the Berea area and could be commuting students. We had received permission to house the participants in the home management house which had six bedrooms and a small apartment for someone on the staff to stay day and night with the women in case they needed help or someone to talk with if they should become homesick. We were delighted when Sidney Farr agreed to be our first "house-sister." Under these arrangements, we could have twelve resident students and two non-residents. They would take their meals in the college cafeteria, use college classroom space for classes, and the college vans for transportation to events on weekends that we felt would strongly enhance the cultural aspect of the program.

As plans progressed, it became obvious that the $14,000 award from the foundation would not cover the cost of the program once we helped the participants with travel expenses and the cost of child care in their home communities—two important factors to be considered. Where was this additional money going to come from? John suggested I ask Rod Bussey for suggestions of possible donors we could approach for additional funds. I was somewhat uncomfortable in this position because I felt as though I was asking for money for myself even though I was taking no salary for directing the program except for expenses I might incur. However, I didn't have much choice and soon learned how "to make the ask." It became easier as I would remind myself that I was really asking for the funds for the women we would help.

Several members of the Berea College Board of Trustees sent generous donations, and finally enough funds were available that we knew we could operate.

In April we had received fifty-eight requests for applications. By the first of May, fourteen women had been selected and we were excitedly awaiting their arrival for our first session, scheduled for June 7 through 27, 1987. An interesting and challenging three-week schedule had been completed.

Finally, the long-anticipated day came and we awaited the arrival of our first class of participants of the New Opportunity School. I don't know who was most nervous, the participants or me. We served punch and cookies, and many advisory board members were at the home management house to welcome the women. How wonderful it was to put faces with the applications we had read and reread.

Of the twelve women attending that first session, two were from Berea, one came from the mountains of North Carolina, and the others were from different locations in eastern Kentucky. Although fourteen women were chosen, much to our disappointment two did not show up. I phoned them all day, wondering where they were, but got no response. Unfortunately, this is a pattern we have experienced often during these twenty-five years and have learned to keep in touch with the women right up to the time of their arrival, asking them if they need anything, how we can help, and encouraging them that they can take this huge step in their lives. How difficult it is for the women to leave home for three weeks when they receive little or no support from husbands or other family members to make this new journey. We learned later that a woman who did not show up was concerned she didn't have proper clothes or luggage to bring her belongings in. Child-care arrangements often fell through at the last minute. Health problems of family members kept the women at home. Sudden car trouble would make the women late so they would make the decision to not come at all.

By mid-afternoon, twelve participants had arrived and had gotten acquainted. Soon after settling in their rooms, Dorothy Coffey spent time with each individual participant interpreting the information from the Strong-Campbell interest inventory and explaining how we had matched information from the inventory to their assigned labor positions. During the next three weeks, the women were given tours of the library by Sidney Farr and Barbara Power, and of the Appalachian Museum, operated by the college at that time but now no longer in existence. Mary Ann Murray taught the first Appalachian Literature course. Janice Blythe gave a seminar on Resource Management. Dorothy Coffey taught classes in job search skills. Gurney Norman taught Creative Writing and by the end of the session, we hoped that each participant could give Gurney something she had written that we would put together in booklet form as a keepsake.

Anita Barker taught self-esteem classes and Diane Kerby led a seminar on women in non-traditional jobs. "Computer Basics" classes were held to give the women courage to perhaps seek further

Loyal Jones, Director of the Berea College Appalachian Center, and author Wilma Dykeman discuss her book *The Tall Woman* in 1990, which was part of required reading for the Appalachian Literature class.

training in computer use when they returned home. Paul Hager coordinated a panel discussion on "Is Further Education in Your Future?" When possible, activities on the college campus such as readings by Wilma Dykeman and Jim Wayne Miller, and a poetry reading by Sidney Farr and Sallie Odom were attended. As in the Danish Folk School tradition of the former Opportunity School, our group also enjoyed an evening of folk dancing. Weekends were spent touring Shakertown, Fort Boonesboro, and traveling to Lexington to a conference for women sponsored by the Kentucky Commission on Women. Before our first graduation at noon on Saturday, June 27, events were held for families of the women, which included a campus tour and a visit to the college planetarium. Looking at that first schedule now, it is amazing that most of the course offerings are still the same—after twenty-five years.

Of those twelve courageous women who came to our first session in 1987, four have died—three of cancer. Knowing the importance of early cancer detection and learning that few of our participants had ever had even a baseline mammogram encouraged us to make sure all women attending our program had a free mammogram. We provided other medical care as needed. In later years of the program, we included an opportunity for a Pap smear, and have always included a class in women's health issues.

As with any new, experimental program, one seeks to improve programs with each session held. The advisory committee met in the fall of 1987 to evaluate and start plans for the next year. Participants had filled out an extensive evaluation form and this information was our basis for making changes for the future as we planned for 1988 and beyond. Fundraising continued, as we approached other foundations through suggestions from the Berea College Development office. Now that we knew the program was of great value to participants, we knew funding had to be secured for the future. Because we had received thirty-one applications and could only take fourteen women, we also had to consider the possibility of two sessions per year in the future.

In spring 1988, the board of the Ford Foundation met in Berea. During the day the board traveled in eastern Kentucky to look at programs they had funded there. In the evenings, they were entertained with dinners at Berea College, including one in the president's home. At that dinner, I was seated beside a program officer of the foundation and over dinner explained the New Opportunity School for Women. The program officer asked what I thought was our greatest need, and I replied that we needed to offer two sessions a year to help more women since we had turned down more than half the women who had applied. I told her that Boone Tavern, owned and operated by Berea College, was willing to give us a good discount on rooms if we held the session in January or February, which would allow us to hold a winter and summer session, and twice as many women could benefit from our program.

"What else do you need?" she asked. I told her that we needed a scholarship fund that our graduates could apply to for financial help as they furthered their education.

"Why don't you send us a proposal?" she asked. Of course, I was delighted and began writing a proposal requesting $50,000 over two years. A new scholarship fund would make up $10,000 of the request, leaving $20,000 a year to operate the new winter session. I was also counting on other donors to continue to donate funds to keep the program going. As I spoke to church and civic groups all over Kentucky, more people were learning about the NOSW and were very generous in their support. As the wife of the president, I was very sensitive to personally raising the funds to keep the program going. I did not want this program to take funds from any other budgeted programs on campus; therefore, much of my time was spent finding donors and foundations to support the NOSW.

Much to the delight of all involved with the New Opportunity School, the Ford Foundation granted $50,000 to us, and we now had the responsibility of planning two sessions a year.

Meanwhile, Brenda Banks, a recent graduate of the NOSW, enrolled at Berea College as a student and asked that her labor position be with the New Opportunity School. Tracy Grubbs had asked for a new assignment better suited to her nursing major. I was delighted with Brenda. She had good organizational skills, great ideas, and having been a participant, she also knew what the program should offer the women. Brenda kept this labor assignment for the three years she attended Berea College and was a wonderful asset to the program and to me.

Our first winter session of the New Opportunity School in 1989 was attended by twelve women. Courses remained essentially the same as the summer schedule. We were thrilled we could offer this special experience to more women.

With each session, the number of graduates of the NOSW increased, and we knew we needed organized follow-up with our graduates. Not a day passed without hearing good news from our participants regarding their accomplishments. We began a newsletter and a yearly reunion. Both have continued and grown these twenty-five years.

Fundraising continued successfully, and the program received much good publicity, including an article in the *New York Times*. This article generated interest in the program throughout the country and resulted in donations of funds and wonderful clothing for our clothes closet.

The article in the *New York Times* was an unexpected bonus for our program. It came about when a reporter came to the house for an appointment with John to interview him about coal mining in Kentucky. John was late. The reporter was unhappy that John wasn't there, so I served him tea and cookies and tried to make conversation. He asked me, "Well, what do you do all day?" That was all he needed to say to get me started. I talked and talked about the NOSW and the needs of Appalachian women. By this point he had started taking notes. At long last, John arrived and the reporter said to me, "I'll be in touch." I really never expected to hear from him again; however, several months later he phoned that he wanted to come to Berea and see the program in action. The resulting article made the front page of the *New York Times* and was wonderfully sensitive to the needs of Appalachian women and specifically how the NOSW was helping meet these needs.

Brenda Banks knew we were always searching for funds, and she came up with the idea of compiling a cookbook to raise funds and to bring our program to the attention of more people. We contacted several businesses that printed cookbooks and chose one, Fundcraft, located in Tennessee. Notices were sent to our graduates and friends to submit recipes. This project generated much interest and was a very successful fundraising project. In fact, a few years later we published a second volume, and that cookbook is still sold at local bookstores. Part of the proceeds from the sale of the cookbook began an emergency fund to make loans to our graduates, which they committed to repay when possible.

Evaluation of our program continued, and after two years a survey was sent to all our graduates to learn what they were doing and how the program had affected their lives. For example, the survey in 1991 of the ninety-two graduates showed that almost 63 percent of the graduates were employed full or part-time and another 25 percent were enrolled in school full or part-time. A survey has been conducted every two years since that time and we are pleased that the survey continues to confirm our high success rate—approximately 75 percent of our graduates are employed or in school!

By 1990, it became obvious that a ten-hour labor student and a part-time program director were not enough staff to run a program that was growing and expanding. Much of my time was spent in fundraising and speaking to clubs and organizations, and I was continuing to participate with John in all activities of Berea College. At one such event at the college, a man in the audience asked what my greatest need was at that moment. I told him that if I didn't get more help, especially secretarial, I didn't know how we could continue to run the program. He asked how much I needed to hire a part-time person and I responded, "$5,000." He said, "You've got it." I was thrilled and immediately hired Connie McLain who wanted only a part-time job because she was enrolled in nursing school as well.

It was an exciting time! *The New York Times* article had brought us to the attention of so many people that the phones were ringing constantly. John, ever helpful, answered and took messages when he was home. One day, he handed me a message that read "Call Sally Jesse Raphael at this number in New York." I had no idea who she was and called the number and asked to speak with her. Complete silence

# Changing Lives in Appalachia

After moving the NOSW office from the President's Home on the Berea College Campus in 1992, the Bond House on Chestnut Street served as headquarters until 1997.

on the other end. Another person came on the line and identified herself as a producer of a television show. They wanted me and two or three of our graduates to appear on their show. I had never seen the program on TV and had no idea what kind of show it was. I was told we would be flown to New York, met at the airport by a limo and driver, housed in an exclusive hotel, receive a makeover, then appear on the show to be interviewed by Sally Jesse herself. I told her I would get back with her and proceeded to ask friends and our advisory board what kind of show this was. My mother–in-law reported the show had naked men on it (apparently the Chippendales); others said the show exploited people and didn't treat them kindly. I finally had a chance to watch it. I called some of our graduates to get their opinion. No one wanted to be on the show, so with thanks I declined this invitation.

The President's Home was getting crowded! There was also a possibility that a graduate student from Eastern Kentucky University would be assigned as an intern with us. Where would we put everyone? The President's Home had so much activity with the New Opportunity School and our usual entertaining for the college that we were getting mixed up about who people were when they appeared at our door.

In fall 1991, a member of the Berea College Board of Trustees, Tom Oliver, and his wife, Dottie, came to Berea to live and volunteer for the college for a semester. Dottie wanted to volunteer at the New Opportunity School, which was great, but where could we put a desk for her? Dottie made it her personal project to find a suitable office for us on campus. On January 30, 1992, we moved out of the president's home and into the Bond House at 213 Chestnut Street, a college-owned older home. This was a great move, giving us more space and allowing people to visit our office more easily. Connie McLain had finished her degree and left the NOSW to go into nursing full-time. Pat Chapin was hired as our first, full-time secretary.

We continued to learn of the many needs of our participants. We learned that once they completed our program and went home to rural areas, it was hard to find jobs. Many of the women were talented in making craft items but had never thought of selling them. In 1990 and for several more years, we partnered with the Mountain Association for Community Economic Development (MACED), based in Berea, to offer day-long workshops on "Starting Your Own Home-Based Business: How to Produce and Sell Your Crafts." It was so well attended we were surprised and overwhelmed. The workshop was open to the graduates of our program and anyone living in the area. The charge of five dollars covered the workshop and the cost of lunch. Close to a hundred people attended each time we offered the workshop, bringing their craft items to be evaluated by employees of the Student Craft Industry of Berea College. Later, we also offered another successful home-based business workshop opportunity with

MACED and the Eastern Kentucky Child Care Coalition on starting a home-based business in licensed childcare. Our relationship with MACED and the support of MACED President, Frank Taylor, started a cooperative partnership of many years.

That same year, we started an organization called "Women for Women" to recognize low-income women whose achievements improved the quality of life for themselves and their families, and to maintain our scholarship fund for our graduates. Membership was open to anyone who wished to pay yearly dues of three dollars. Members were encouraged to donate to the scholarship fund according to their ability to do so. The first year, 120 joined and raised about $2,500 in funds for scholarships. At the reunion that year, Linda Baxter Linville and Clarice Zureick were honored as "Women of Achievement," beginning another aspect of our program that still continues. Through the years, other awards were begun such as the John B. Stephenson Loyalty Award; the Joy Award given by Janet Tronc and her family; the Janie Polk Scholarship awarded by her family; and the Evan Frankel scholarships. Generous donors and foundations continue to support this fund.

By this time, the annual budget was $50,000 a year. Foundations were interested in the program and we began to receive funds from the Berea College Appalachian Fund, the Steele-Reese Foundation, the Second Foundation, the Aaronson Foundation, the Cralle and Gheens Foundations of Louisville, and many individual donors. Our volunteer, Dottie Oliver, and I traveled to New York City along with two of our graduates, Katie Rollins and Garnet Sexton, to visit foundations to ask for funding. Individual donors paid for the trip. It was deemed very successful for future funding, as well as an educational trip for our two graduates who had neither been to New York nor flown on an airplane. We took a train to upper New York state to speak to a Berea College alumni gathering, which was also a valuable experience for all of us.

During these early years of the program, there was much interest

TWENTY-FIVE YEARS of HISTORY

NOSW counselor Anita Barker, center, presents the first recipients of the Women of Achievement award with their plaques in 1991. At left is Clarice Zureick and at right is Linda Baxter Linville.

in the participants, their courage, and their accomplishments. Many newspapers and magazines wrote stories about the program that created exciting contacts and opportunities for those of us working hard to keep it going. I must admit there were times when we started a session not knowing how we would pay for it, but we had faith that the funds would come in, and they always did. Support from the college was exceptional, and we were almost never turned down when we asked people to teach, host an intern, or provide their expertise.

Women's organizations all over the region wanted to know how they could be of help. The Berea Chapter of the American Association of University Women provided a meal and program for each session and have continued to do so for these twenty-five years! The Berea Younger Woman's Club always provided a social event and dinner for the women each session.

From the beginning of the program, we collected good used clothing appropriate for interviews and work. We wanted to ensure that all graduates would leave with an interview suit to accompany our instructions regarding job interviews. Makeovers provided by local beauty salons and a beauty school provided the women with self-confidence for job interviews. Women's groups and other organizations from across Kentucky and many individuals provided good gently used business clothes for our clothing closet.

The Bluegrass Home Economists were great supporters. The Riverside Business and Professional Woman's Club in Louisville, as well as the Berea Business and Professional Woman's Club, were especially interested in providing interview suits and continued that project as part of their club's outreach for many years. Many women, men, and couples sent donations, large and small. We could not have existed without our generous donors throughout the years.

An attorney in Washington, D.C., Kathy Vagt, started our Christmas project. She sent scarves and jewelry donated by attorneys and staff at her firm. Local volunteers brought paper and boxes and wrapped the items, placed them in padded bags, and each women received a Christmas gift from the NOSW. As more and more women graduated from our program, we asked other churches and organizations to donate gifts. We continued this project for many years until we could no longer afford the postage for mailing the gifts as it was costing more than $500 a year. Reluctantly, we discontinued the project; however, we have continued to mail birthday and Christmas cards to our graduates. One year, 1991, we received extra funds to give each woman a subscription to the *Appalachian Heritage Magazine*, published by Berea College.

One of our great NOSW supporters was Alex Haley, who was a trustee at Berea College. I asked him if he would ever be available to be at our graduation to present certificates. He was able to work out his schedule to do so, and as he met the women and admired their abilities, he wanted to do more for the program. Each session, he invited us to his home in Norris, Tennessee, for lunch and a tour of his farm. He made a special point to be with us but occasionally he could not. Even when he was not there, his staff treated us to a meal and made us feel at home. Once, Alex even provided us with music by a string quartet from Knoxville; they performed while we

Author Alex Haley, center, frequently hosted a tour for the NOSW women at his farm near Norris, Tennessee. It was a special and inspiring moment for the women every year until his death in 1992.

had lunch. A great supporter of education, he would talk with the women about the importance of staying in school and related many inspiring stories. We were with him at his farm two weeks before his untimely death on February 10, 1992. A memorial service at Danforth Chapel was held while the NOSW participants were still on campus. We all loved him and admired his generous spirit. His death was a loss to the entire world.

Wilma Dykeman, also a member of the Berea College Board of Trustees, often talked with the NOSW participants about writing and especially about her book, *The Tall Woman*, which the women read and discussed in our Appalachian Literature classes. She would sometimes meet us at Alex Haley's home, driving from her home in Newport, Tennessee. We would sit around the big fireplace and listen to all her wisdom as she discussed writing and her life growing up in the mountains of North Carolina.

For several years, Stella Parton, sister of Dolly Parton, attended our graduations and one year was an inspirational speaker. She enjoyed coming to Berea the evening before graduation to lead a workshop, "Beauty on a Budget and Self-esteem is Free." Participants enjoyed talking with Stella about their futures and listened carefully to her ideas for makeup, clothes, and building self-confidence.

Stella Parton speaks at a NOSW event in Knoxville, Tennessee, on June 28, 2012. (© Ben Poage)

By 1993 it had become obvious that a part-time

career/education counselor would be a great addition to our staff. As we continued to receive more applications than we could admit, our advisory committee had concerns for all the women in eastern Kentucky who could not come to our program but still needed advice on career and educational planning. Additional funds were raised to create a new position. We hired Caroline Francis as our first career/education counselor. She worked part-time at the NOSW office and held workshops for women in eastern Kentucky about writing effective resumes, interviewing skills, self-esteem development, time management, and communication skills. These workshops were well received. In the first six-month period, thirty-one women had one or more sessions, totaling eighty-five appointments with our career counselor. We were pleased with the opportunity to expand

As part of the leadership development component, the women always take a trip to the State Capitol and the Governor's Mansion. First Lady Judi Patton, center, arranged to meet the participants and staff and pose for photos. (© Staff, Governor's Office)

our services in this direction. Caroline also started a Career Success League, a support group for women in our region looking for employment. It was held in our office every other Tuesday evening.

At the same time, a graduate student at Eastern Kentucky University, Teresa Johnson (Libby), was assigned to our office as an intern. I had recently attended a leadership program for women in Kentucky and had realized that the women needing more leadership development skills were really the women attending the NOSW, as they had never considered themselves leaders. Teresa began to do library research and learned that no programs existed that we could use. The two of us developed a leadership component to add to our three-week session. Classes were held to help participants recognize their leadership skills and abilities, including public speaking, how to become a member of a board of an organization in the community, how to conduct meetings, how city and county governments worked, and how to use this information to help low-income people find resources to improve their lives. We learned also that fewer people in Kentucky voted than any state and that women voted less often than men. We encouraged our participants to register to vote and to vote at every election.

An important part of the leadership experience was a trip to the State Capitol in Frankfort. In 1994, Libby Jones, wife of Governor Brereton Jones, invited us to enjoy the afternoon at the Governor's Mansion where we received an informative tour and enjoyed tea and cookies. Later, Judi Patton, wife of Governor Paul Patton, and more recently Jane Beshear, wife of Governor Steve Beshear, continued this important event.

Two of our graduates have run for public office. Recently we heard from a graduate who had been asked to be on the board of a local domestic abuse shelter. We were thrilled as we knew how important this opportunity could be for her. Many of our graduates have assumed leadership roles in their home communities because they received encouragement through our classes.

In 1993, we received funds to offer internships in our office to give our graduates without jobs an opportunity to get work experience. We interviewed the women who applied and chose six to spend two months each in a paid internship with us. Most of these women were later offered jobs or went on to school for more training.

In fall 1993, my husband made the decision to retire as president of Berea College for health reasons. He had been diagnosed a few years earlier with leukemia, but it was well under control. However, John felt strongly that he needed to get more rest, and wanted to have more time for writing and perhaps consulting. In June, we moved into our own home on Jackson Street in Berea, where we planned to live for the rest of our lives. I felt strongly about living in Berea and continuing my work with the NOSW. On August 1, 1994, John retired, and we took a group of Berea College alumni and friends on a study tour of Scotland. Harvard University officials invited John to teach a class there. In September 1994, we moved to Cambridge for a semester. Caroline Francis became the acting director of the NOSW while I was away, and we hired a new secretary, Kim McGuire. I left knowing that the program was in good hands.

John was excited to be on the Harvard University campus. We rented a small, furnished apartment and loved roaming around the area, visiting the museums in Boston and attending a Boston Symphony concert. I had a vague uneasiness that John wasn't feeling well. In October, after teaching only three weeks, John became ill and was hospitalized. After many tests he was diagnosed with a rare virus of the brain. Despite excellent medical care, we were told there was nothing that could be done for this condition and that at the most he might have six months to live. We returned in November by air ambulance to Berea. John died December 6, 1994.

There was so much sadness and grief in our family, and people all over the world sent letters expressing their sorrow and their love of John. Our family and close friends were shocked and devastated. John was only fifty-seven and had so much to give to the world. I was fortunate to have a good friend, Rev. Randy Osborne, our campus minister, help me through this very hard time. Our children were wonderful. Although they lived out of town, they came to Berea as often as possible as we shared in our grief and loss. Eventually, they all moved back to Kentucky.

I did not go back to work until March 1995. Caroline and Kim continued to work hard for the NOSW, assuring its continued success.

On April 25, 1995, graduates and staff of the NOSW planted a tree in the yard of the Bond House in memory of John. Appropriately, it was a Scottish Pine. The plaque reads:

> In memory of John B. Stephenson
> "Mr. Jane"
> He touched our hearts,
> Rekindled Our Spirits
> And gave us new opportunities to explore.

Through the years, many of our graduates traveled with me to talk to groups and tell their life stories. People hearing them speak would often ask if I was writing down their stories. I began writing a book about our graduates' lives even before John's death, but it had been slow getting started. John had encouraged me to write, as had Frank Taylor, the President of MACED, and Ron Fouts, a Berea College graduate and publisher who had agreed to publish my book. After John's death, I knew I had to finish this book as a special tribute to him and his love of the New Opportunity School and the many women he had met. He had on occasion taught the Appalachian Literature classes and especially loved taking trips with us and driving the van. The women loved to be in his van, as he would stop for garage/yard sales along the way. They called him *Mr. Jane*, a title he didn't seem to mind and one that was a refreshing change from his usual *Mr. President*.

In this time of grief and sorrow, I found that writing these true stories of the lives of several of our graduates gave me the courage to continue my own life and work. In 1995, *Courageous Paths* was published. Gurney Norman, who has been so faithful to our program throughout the years, and who knew the women well from his work with them, agreed to write a special introduction. Also included in the book was an article Rudy Abramson wrote that was originally published in the *Appalachian Heritage* magazine. Rudy, a Washington correspondent for *The Los Angeles Times* newspaper, spent a year teaching at Berea College and had come to know and understand the New Opportunity School. He wrote articles about the program for *The Los Angeles Times, Smithsonian* magazine and other publications. More than 6,000 copies of *Courageous Paths* have been sold to supporters and friends, or given to our participants.

Several people sent copies of *Courageous Paths* to Oprah Winfrey, suggesting it for one of her book club selections. Although that never happened, I believe that the book and Gwyn Hyman Rubio's mention of the NOSW when her book, *Icy Sparks,* was chosen by Oprah's Book Club, played a large role in our being selected to appear on *The Oprah Winfrey Show* and receive her "Use Your Life Award." Gwyn and her husband, Angel, have been special friends to the NOSW, and our participants love listening to Gwyn talk about *Icy Sparks* as they read and discuss her book in the Appalachian Literature classes.

A friend who taught in the theater department at Lees-McRae College in Banner Elk, North Carolina, read *Courageous Paths* and we discussed adapting it for the stage. Kim Stinson worked hard to keep the play true to the book, using the exact words of the characters. Kim spent hours writing the play. How excited we all were when it premiered at the theater in the Berea Community School April 28 - 30, 2004. The theater was filled for all performances, and some people even saw the play twice. Eddie Kennedy directed it, and many of the actors came from the Berea Community Theater group that Eddie directed in Berea for several years. The following July, the play was performed at Lees-McRae College for four nights. Because the space was smaller, Kim rewrote the script, adapting it for a limited space. For these performances, Kim also directed the play. The performers included professionals who were at Lees-McRae for summer theater performances as well as Lees-McRae students, and one performer, Patty Boyce, came from Berea to repeat her Berea performance. More recently, an even shorter version was successfully adapted and directed by Deborah Martin and performed by Berea College students for a fundraising event at Boone Tavern.

Beth Wright, a friend of my daughter, Rebecca, read Rebecca's copy of *Courageous Paths*. She was touched by the story of Ada. Both Beth and Rebecca had been students together at the University of North Carolina at Greensboro working toward master's degrees in dance. Later, Beth asked permission to set the story of Ada to dance for an alumni concert at UNC-G. Permission was granted, and Rebecca and I enjoyed a trip to Greensboro to see a touching, emotional performance.

After John's death, I became totally involved with the New Opportunity School. There was so much to be done and always more funds to raise. We sought more ways to help the women, especially financially. We rented space at a local antiques mall and featured craft items made by the participants to help them generate additional income. For a short period, with the help of Ron Fouts, we started the Mountain Box Company. A nonprofit company in Lexington made boxes, NOSW graduates in the Berea area decorated them which we sold through local shops. The women were paid for their time but none of these projects really brought in enough funds to make them worth the time and effort so they were eventually discontinued.

This was a time of creativity, of trying new ways to help our graduates become successful. It was an exciting time to watch the changes and the growth of the women we were working with at the New Opportunity School for Women.

## NEW PATHS FOR THE NEW OPPORTUNITY SCHOOL

By 1996, the NOSW was running smoothly, funds were coming in, women were successfully becoming employed and educated, and the program was becoming well known locally and nationally. Berea College was undergoing a new strategic plan generated by the new president, Larry Shinn. The NOSW was originally placed administratively under the auspices of the Berea College Appalachian Center, directed at that time by Loyal Jones, a great supporter of the NOSW and a man who understood our mission as he had spent his life working in and for the Appalachian region. His replacement, Gordon McKinney, asked for a meeting with me at which time he indicated that our program needed to be more focused on providing educational opportunities for the traditional Berea College undergraduate student. One section of the report of the strategic plan, "Being and Becoming," deals with the place of outreach as part of Berea College and recommends that:

> Berea College should (a) develop, primarily through undergraduate education, service-oriented leaders for Appalachia and for the other places where our students will live; (b) take advantage of the learning and service opportunities that are abundant throughout the region through the integration of curricular, co-curricular, and out-reach programs; (c) place all of Berea's outreach activities within the learning/service context and be willing to fund them." One way to accomplish this goal is to "integrate service to the region into our curricular and co-curricular, and out-reach programs; (c) place all of Berea's outreach activities within the learning/service context and be willing to fund them." One way to accomplish this goal is to "integrate service to the region into our curricular and co-curricular programs so that servicing the region is

interwoven with our educational mission." (Quoted from pages 35 - 36 of the Strategic Plan, "Being and Becoming.")

I went through the college catalogue reading each course description and thinking through ways the NOSW could involve students. We had already advertised our program extensively to the students, asking them to inform their mothers and older sisters of the NOSW. We always accepted mothers of Berea College students when possible and appropriate to do so. At that time, twenty mothers of Berea College students had completed our program successfully.

I found many opportunities for Berea College students to learn from the NOSW and created a lengthy proposal to address how the NOSW could interweave our program with the educational mission of Berea College. With input from Berea College faculty, ten courses were selected to develop components of the courses that would relate to the NOSW. For example: NUR212: Nursing and the Childbearing Family focused on women's reproductive health with health promotion and wellness emphasized. Working with the instructor, we proposed that a women's health issues component be added to their course content whereby the students would hold a "health fair" for participants of the NOSW. The nursing students would provide screenings such as blood pressure, breast self-exam demonstrations, and health education such as exercise and diet information.

Nine other courses were developed for classes in Sociology, English, Health, Women's Studies, Family and Child Development, and others. A list of fifteen cooperative possibilities were developed that included methods to integrate the NOSW into the learning environment of Berea College. For example, one suggestion was: The NOSW staff and graduates of the school provide informational lectures on the status of women in Appalachia for classroom lectures, convocations, and co-curricular programs and encourage, when appropriate, that NOSW graduates be admitted to Berea College for further study either with "special student" status or in the regular curriculum.

In April, I gave a seven-page proposal to President Shinn. Later, I received a letter from him in which he indicated that we should consider if our "goals for the NOSW would be better realized in continuing its mission as it is and consequently, making clear its independent status from Berea College."

Through meetings and letters exchanged, it was made quite clear by President Shinn that if the New Opportunity School remained with Berea College, its mission possibly could be changed dramatically. The president indicated that a committee would be appointed to look carefully at the New Opportunity School to be sure it fit with the new strategic plan, and if it didn't we would be told to change our program. An example he gave of a possibility of a new design was that he was concerned that the retention rate of Berea College students was low and that perhaps our assignment would be to work with the families of students who were leaving the college without graduating. In no way would he assure me that the program would continue our mission of helping low-income Appalachian women. He wrote, "the implementation committee might recommend that the program continue 'as is;' the implementation committee might recommend that the program be modified in specific ways that the committee and the College faculty endorse; or the implementation committee might recommend that the program be ended and that the financial and/or other College resources formerly allocated to the program be used for other purposes." We were also told that after the review process, we would no longer have the option to leave Berea College. In other words, we had to face the "now or never" reality.

The NOSW had never been officially placed in the budget of the college, and it was my job to raise our operating costs year after year. President Shinn informed me that my fundraising for the NOSW, even though approved through the college development office, was getting in the way of the fundraising by the president. I was amazed—our little program that cost only about $100,000 a year was a fundraising threat to the rest of Berea College?

I was stunned. I immediately called together our advisory board. One member wrote she was "reluctant to risk modifications or the death of a program that has statistical evidence to document its tremendous success." Many made appointments with the president and wrote letters supporting the NOSW remaining at Berea College. After discussion and careful contemplation, our advisory board made the decision that our program was too important, too successful, to take a chance that it would be changed, and that our only alternative would be to leave Berea College.

At this time, MACED made a generous offer that we join them as an affiliate of their organization. This was a life-saving offer because at that time we didn't have our own 501(c)(3) nonprofit designation letter from the IRS and therefore could not even accept donations. Other advantages to joining with MACED were enrollment in their retirement fund, the expertise of an accountant, a motor pool and generally the support and welcome of their president, Don Harker. It was with great sadness in November 1996 that we left Berea College administratively, although we had negotiated to rent our college-owned office for another year and could continue to rent classroom space and other facilities in the manner of other off-campus programs, such as Elderhostel.

Our advisory board became a decision-making Board of Directors. New members were added. Our first president of this new board was Barbara Power, with Anita Barker serving at vice president. Frank Souther was treasurer, and new board member, Virginia Underwood, became secretary. Virginia, an attorney with experience in applying for 501(c)(3) nonprofit designation, spent hours helping us design by-laws, form a charter, and file appropriate papers. In record time, we received our nonprofit status. Many articles were written in newspapers all over the country, donors were informed of our move, and our program continued with only a momentary hitch. In fact, our supporters rallied around us and came forward with more help than ever before in many and varied ways. The caring and supportive atmosphere at MACED was wonderful for all of us. Many new ideas and bonds were formed that still exist today, even though several years later the NOSW chose to become independent.

During this time, we were also looking for new office quarters. The Bond House had been so perfectly located with sufficient space for our growing clothing closet as well as offices for staff. Fortunately, we learned that the parsonage at First Christian Church was going to be available to rent as their minister had bought a home of his own in Berea. They were committed to renting this space to a nonprofit group, and keeping the rent affordable for this type organization. It was just across the street from us on Chestnut Street.

The house was perfect for our needs, including a very large finished basement for our clothing closet, storage, and perhaps even meeting space if needed. The church also invited us to use their education building for meetings. It became a real advantage for us to hold our yearly reunions as well as board meetings in the church. Later, in a joint project between the church and the NOSW, we enclosed the carport and made a computer lab. We had been teaching our computer classes at the college and at the local high school, and our classes had to be scheduled around the computer lab availability. Enclosing the carport was a real bonus, giving us a room that could be used for many other classes as well.

In the spring of 2000, the Bennett Center in London, Kentucky, approached us about holding one of our sessions there. The space was perfect as the Bennett Center was formerly Sue Bennett College, with dorm space, classroom facilities, and a cafeteria. Sue Bennett College began as a school for women. A United Methodist Women's organization in New York, part of the General Board of Global Ministries, had been owners of the property for over 100 years, and wanted to continue to help women and children. Our program fit well into their mission. It was a hard decision to start a program there because the location was almost an hour south of Berea, and we had very little staff and certainly no funds to begin such a program.

After much consideration by our board, a donor coming forth with funds, and a large commitment of in-kind services and facilities from the Bennett Center, we agreed to experiment with one session in October 2000. Women's groups in London helped decorate dull dorm rooms, provide evening meals, and generally be supportive. Especially helpful were the four NOSW board members from London who introduced us to donors and held teas to generate interest. The session was very successful, although it was hard for the NOSW staff to keep the Berea office going and also run the session in London. The participants chosen for the program were thrilled and have been very successful in their lives. Two years later, another successful session was held in London; however, it was getting harder and harder to raise funds for both the London and Berea sessions and our board reluctantly made the decision not to continue the London program.

Nineteen-ninety-seven was an eventful year. As we were preparing for the winter session, I received a call from Linda Saether, a producer with Cable News Network (CNN). I had met her a year or so earlier when they were briefly on the Berea College campus. She had asked me several questions about the New Opportunity School, but I wasn't sure anything would come of it. She phoned to say they wanted to do a story on our program. I talked with her about confidentiality of our graduates, how some people might not want to be on camera, how she must assure us that the women interviewed would feel good about themselves, and that there would be no negative stereotyping of the Appalachian region. She understood and agreed. They arrived in late February, attended classes, filmed the participants of our winter session as they received makeovers at the Eastern School of Hair Design in Richmond, and filmed women in their internships. They even traveled to Lee and Estill counties to film NOSW graduates who had started their own businesses and interviewed a graduate who was in college. The experience was very positive, and we had much respect for the film and production crew.

We anxiously waited to hear when we would be on CNN. When the date in April finally arrived, several of us gathered around my TV at home on a Sunday morning at nine a.m. to see the program. The first thing we heard were hound dogs barking, chickens crowing, and a photo of a dilapidated house. "OH NO," we all gasped simultaneously, but then we heard the voice saying "things are changing in Appalachia," and the scene immediately faded into a beautiful farm scene and then to the campus of Berea College and a truly wonderful story that gave us great publicity and made us proud. The production crew had come through, and we were pleased with our first foray into national television.

As you can imagine, we received many phone calls after the program aired, mostly from people wanting to know how to start a similar program in their community or if they could come to our program even though they didn't live in Appalachia.

About this same time, I was having struggles in my own life. My mother, who lived alone in North Carolina, was diagnosed with Alzheimer's Disease, and I was making frequent trips to see her. I was still grieving the loss of my husband of thirty-two years, and fundraising was becoming more and more time-consuming. I began to feel that I was not able to give to the NOSW the time it deserved and that my own health was being affected by the long hours I was giving to the program and frequent drives to North Carolina. Caroline Francis was still our career/education counselor, and Kim was taking on more responsibilities in program management. We had enough funds to operate for two years, and we were getting ready to move into new office space. Our arrangement as an affiliate with MACED was working well. Caroline had done an excellent job as acting director when I was away several months so perhaps she could become the director. It seemed like a good time for me to step down as director of the NOSW. I was still feeling the emotional sadness connected with leaving our birthing place—Berea College. Could I really leave this program that had been my life-blood for so many years? We had just celebrated our tenth anniversary with a great program of celebration with graduates and donors, and the program had taken on a life of its own.

It was a terribly hard decision for me, and I still remember the shock on the faces of our board members when I told them what I felt I must do. I suggested Caroline as the new director, and, after much thought and deliberation, the board accepted my resignation and asked that I remain on the board and assume the title of founder/ advisor. Caroline was made director and Kim was given more responsibilities and a new title. Barbara Kinkaid was selected as the new career/education counselor. I promised that I would stay closely connected to the program, and especially continue to help raise funds and be involved as much as needed.

My life changed in many ways during this period, but I never lost touch with my love and close affiliation with the NOSW. I moved my mother from North Carolina to Kentucky—a decision that was especially hard for her and emotional for our family. Kentucky had become my home, and I believed my work was here. My children had also moved back to Kentucky from Atlanta, Georgia; Jackson, Wyoming; and Greensboro, North Carolina. I was a proud grandmother for the first time.

In 1997, I started a part-time seasonal job with the Steele-Reese Foundation as their Appalachian director. I had great admiration for this Foundation. I learned about them when they donated funds to the NOSW and learned of their giving history in eastern Kentucky, western North Carolina, and eastern Tennessee. They needed someone familiar with the region to accept proposals, do site visits, attend their yearly board meetings in New York, and work with their trustees as they considered nonprofits that would receive their grants. I was pleased to have this opportunity to continue to help people in our region and still have time to volunteer my services to the NOSW as needed while also taking care of my mother and enjoying my family.

The New Opportunity School was growing and changing. Caroline had been directing the program and fundraising. Eventually funds became available to hire a full-time person for the fundraising and public relations work that was needed. Amy Harmon, a Berea College graduate who had worked in development at the college, became our development and public relations director.

In 2000, I made the decision to move to Lexington, where I had previously lived for eighteen years and where my children were now living and working. I could also find more and better services and living conditions for my mother. I could still work out of my home office in Lexington for the Steele-Reese Foundation. After fifteen years, leaving Berea and my friends was very hard because our plan had been to stay in Berea for the rest of our lives. Looking back upon this time, it was difficult but it was the right decision for me.

By this time, Caroline and her husband had adopted a baby, and she left the NOSW to be a full-time mother. Amy Harmon became executive director of the NOSW. Kim McGuire Short became program director after serving in various capacities for several years. After Barbara Kincaid's resignation to take a full-time job, Barbara Miles was hired as our career counselor. When she was offered a job at Berea College, she decided she wanted to advance in her career by taking that job. Later, Beverly Stamper filled this position briefly. In 2002, Stephanie Beard became our career/education counselor and has counseled the NOSW women for several years as they seek new jobs. She has also conducted numerous workshops throughout eastern Kentucky to help us serve additional women. These workshops have served as an excellent source for recruitment to our program. The Appalachian Regional Commission also contracted with us to teach leadership workshops in distressed counties in eastern Kentucky.

In winter 2003, during a record-breaking ice storm that covered and immobilized the Lexington area, I received a phone call that seemed a little strange. The person on the phone identified herself as from a television program that was well known and she wanted to ask some questions about me and about the NOSW. I answered as best I could. One question was, "Would you object to a personal background check?" I said "No, that would be fine, but why is that needed?" "We will get back with you," was the only answer I got. I quickly called the NOSW office and talked with Amy, who had received a similar call.

Later that day, I received a phone call from a man in Louisville asking me if I could meet him the next day at our office in Berea to discuss my background check. He still could not tell me what this was about. We were in the middle of an ice storm. I didn't know if I could get to Berea, but I told him I would try. This was getting stranger all the time. He was a very nice man who, as a retired FBI agent, was part of a security company that worked for various "famous" people to do background checks. I knew we were involved in something big, and we were all making guesses about what could possibly be happening.

Apparently, I passed the background check, the NOSW office and staff passed his scrutiny, and people he talked with in Berea must have given good reports. The next day I received a phone call from a producer of Oprah's TV show telling me that I had been selected as an Oprah Angel and would receive the "Use Your Life Award" and $100,000 for the NOSW. A production crew would like to arrive by the middle of the next week.

What excitement! And a mixture of unbelief! Was Oprah coming to Berea? How would we spend the $100,000 award coming to the NOSW from Oprah's foundation? I was pretty calm until I learned there were twenty million viewers of her program daily! Panic set in! What would I wear? What if I said something wrong? Could my family, the NOSW staff, some of our graduates go with me to Chicago? What would the production crew be like? What did they want to film? Who did they want to talk with?

When we watch a program like Oprah's, it looks so easy. We never think about the hours of research and the days of filming and editing that must occur before the program is aired. We learned how professional the crew is at the level of a show like Oprah's. They were wonderfully supportive of the women they wanted to film. They loved our program, our staff, the college campus, and the beauty of Berea and the surrounding area. After five days, we really hated for them to leave. The producer, Jill Adams, stayed to attend our winter session graduation. I introduced her, saying only that she was a guest with an announcement to make. When she told the 150 people gathered to honor our graduates that she was from the Oprah show and that they could expect to see us on a segment of the show in the near future, screams and applause erupted. It was unreal.

Finally we got the word that we would be going to Chicago on March 10 to appear on the show on March 11, 2003. I would be on the show, and tickets were given to my family, several graduates, and the NOSW staff. We quickly made reservations at the Omni Hotel, and people started making plans to drive or fly to Chicago while we kept calling the producers for one more ticket. About thirty representatives of the NOSW went to Chicago one way or another and enjoyed a great two days.

As promised, Oprah sent a limo to the hotel to pick me up, along with all my baggage, as I would be going on to the airport from the show. It was three degrees and windy. I have never been so cold in my life and totally subdued. Upon arriving, I was taken to a little room to sit by myself until eventually someone arrived to do my makeup and hair. I couldn't see what she was doing but had decided when she left the room if I didn't like what she was doing to my hair I would fix it myself. Well, that didn't happen. My hair was sprayed with something so strong I couldn't move even one hair into another place. So much for any hair do-overs I might have in mind. I guess that had been tried before!

Jane Stephenson proudly displays her "Use Your Life Award." (© David Stephenson)

It seemed like hours before I was brought to a seat in the front row of the audience. I had no idea when they would get to our part of the show. As it turned out, we were the last ones to be honored. On a large screen was our story—the first time we had seen how our program was represented. Then Oprah came down into the audience to give me the award, give me a hug, and for me to thank her in a wobbly voice with tears in my eyes. The cheering team we had brought with us went wild, and we were all thrilled and honored. Afterwards I had my photo taken with Oprah and talked with her a little more before being whisked away to talk with the producers and sign forms regarding our $100,000 award. Next stop was the airport and home after a thrilling and exhausting day.

A few months before all this excitement, the NOSW had developed our own Web site which got about fifty hits a week. During the first week after the *Oprah* show was aired, we received over 12,000 hits and an unknown number of E-mails. Most people wanted to come to the NOSW, and others wanted to know how to start a similar program. For months we E-mailed and talked with people!

One very sad note was that one of our participants featured on the show, Libby Chenault, who was shown at her internship at Boone Tavern (where she was later hired), was diagnosed with breast cancer. She fought courageously until her death in 2006. This was another reminder that we must continue to make available mammograms and Pap smears to the women in our program for early diagnosis of cancer. Over these twenty-five years, twenty-five of our participants have died, about half from cancer that was detected too late. We are always aware of the poor health of the women in our program because few have had the funds or the insurance to see doctors or have tests that could save their lives. Several years ago, one woman became ill during the NOSW program and was admitted to the hospital with a blood clot in her leg. She told us later that she would not have received treatment had she been at home because she had no insurance or money for doctors. She said, "Most likely I would have died."

Due to the publicity from our appearance on *Oprah*, a call came from *People* magazine asking if they could come to Berea to do a story. They wanted to feature one woman who would agree to be the focus of the story. We found several who would agree to talk to the reporter and photographer when they arrived. Diana Smallwood, who had graduated that summer, was featured. The article included photos of Diana, her children, the NOSW staff, myself, and volunteers. It was well received after publication in the August 18, 2003, issue of *People* magazine.

An important result of this publicity was that our graduates knew with certainty that they were honored for having the courage to make a life-change by leaving their homes, families, and communities to venture out to Berea and a new life! They were the real heroes.

One day during this time, Amy received a phone call from the producers of the *John Walsh Show* asking about the New Opportunity School. Most people associate John with his show *America's Most Wanted* which came about after the murder of his son, Adam. Not many of us knew he also had an early morning talk show as well. He and his producers had decided to have a show he called *Unsung Heroes* to feature unknown people in small communities across America. He called to invite me and one of our graduates to come to New York and appear on his show the next week. I had never seen the show but after quickly viewing it knew it would be an excellent one for us. A few days later, NOSW graduate George Ann Lakes, who had recently received her master's degree from the University of Kentucky, Amy Harmon, and I boarded a plane for New York. After arriving at the studio, we were excited as John came in to talk with each of us who were to be on his show. First, George Ann came on the set and told her story, then I was brought on to talk about starting the program, our mission, and how many women had become successful because of their participation in the NOSW. After the show we had photos made of us with John. Later we learned that this was John's last show, as NBC had made a decision to take it off the air. We had not known this at the time, but later felt honored to be on his very last show. I have great admiration for John, his special treatment of us, and his down-to-earth personality. We received many E-mails and inquiries about the NOSW after this program but, because his show was not continued by the network, we never received our own tape of the show. We were all very sad that the American public had not supported such a positive show.

Changes were taking place within the NOSW structure. Debbie King had joined the staff in 2003 as a part-time administrative assistant and brought important new skills to the job. New board members joined us and others left when their terms expired. New instructors

NOSW Graduate George Ann Lakes, left, and Founder Jane Stephenson pose with John Walsh after appearing on his television show in 2004. (© Amy Harmon)

came to teach classes, but many people continued to teach year after year. For example, Gurney Norman taught every session for twenty-five years except for one when he was in Italy for a conference. Janie Polk has been teaching our self-esteem classes for years and Judy Halstead has taught computer basics for ten years. Many donors have supported us continually for these twenty-five years and many clubs, churches, and other organizations have continued their interest and contributions.

The NOSW has constantly tried new and innovative ideas that would help our graduates. One example, a project conceived and coordinated by Debra Hille, was an exhibit by the Berea Arts Council of "self-portraits" by our participants. Debra held an instructional retreat, then worked for four months with the women attending the retreat to design self-portraits. At the opening reception at the Berea Arts Council office, over 170 people attended and honored the twelve women who participated and showed their artwork. The project was dedicated to Emma Angel McIntire, one of our deceased graduates, and her artwork was gathered from family and friends to be featured at the show.

Another learning experience for twelve of our graduates occurred through a grant from the Kellogg Foundation. An offer was made to our graduates to apply for a special fundraising opportunity. Several applied and twelve were chosen to attend fundraising workshops where they learned how to raise funds for the NOSW as well as for projects in their own communities. The final event of this project was a fundraising trip to New York City to meet with foundations and donors in that area, as well as attend cultural events.

The Kellogg Foundation has always been very supportive of special learning activities and even provided funds to hold leadership workshops for those women who had graduated from the NOSW prior to our beginning the leadership component of our three-week program. Women from the first several years of the program were given an opportunity to attend several weekend workshops in which we covered the same materials that women were now learning in the three-week sessions. Attendees gave high marks to these workshops and after one such event, one woman ran for a public office. Although she didn't win, she was not discouraged and indicated she would try again in the future.

From the many E-mails we have received from our TV, magazine, and newspaper publicity, we know how much our program is needed all over the United States. Our program has been so successful in Berea, why not try it in other places as well? We were always aware of our concern for and mission to help change the lives of women, especially in Appalachia. With the Appalachian region covering parts of twelve states and all of West Virginia, there must be many more women needing our program. Could we expand to other locations?

## LEADING THE NEW OPPORTUNITY SCHOOL INTO THE FUTURE

Over the years, the inquiries that arrived by phone and E-mail reinforced our awareness of the need for the NOSW in Kentucky and in other Appalachian states. Expanding the program beyond Berea seemed like a much-needed progression in our efforts to help low-income women across the Appalachian region. Expansion was on my mind when a good friend with the Kellogg Foundation, Frank Taylor, visited me at my summer home in Banner Elk, North Carolina, in 2003. Frank asked how many women had come from North Carolina to the Kentucky program. I thought over the years perhaps fifteen had ventured that far from home. (Our research shows that most of our participants are not willing to travel more than two hours from home to attend a program.)

"Why not start a program in North Carolina?" he asked. I became immediately excited and said, "And the perfect place is right here at Lees-McRae College." The mission of the college since its beginning in 1900 has always been to educate the youth of the mountains. Lees-McRae is a small Presbyterian Liberal Arts college with an emphasis on service/learning. The motto is, "In the mountains, Of the mountains, For the mountains." As a graduate of Lees-McRae myself, I knew it was an ideal location for our first expansion site.

Frank indicated that we might be able to receive start-up funds from the Kellogg Foundation if the college could match them. He suggested Lees-McRae send a proposal. Over the next week or two, I talked with the president of the college, Earl Robinson, and various staff in the advancement office to see how much support could be generated. There was much excitement about this possibility from several Lees-McRae faculty and staff, especially from Stephanie Keener, the director of the John B. Stephenson Center for Appalachian and Comparative Highland studies on campus. (My late husband, John, had begun his teaching career in 1961 at Lees-McRae College, where I was also teaching, and John always credited his years at Lees-McRae for his life focus on the Appalachian region.)

Back in Berea, the news of a possible expansion site created great excitement among the board of directors of the New Opportunity School. They appointed a new committee, the expansion committee, led by board member Janet Tronc. There were so many questions. Would this be like a franchise? How would the legal status of another site be designed? How could we be sure that new programs would follow our original guidelines? How would fundraising work between the two sites? Most of all, how could the new site maintain its own identity yet be true to the mission of the original program? Most of the people on the committee had never been to Banner Elk, so they traveled there for a couple of days to brainstorm, see facilities, meet people at Lees-McRae, and generally get acquainted. The visitors from Berea included NOSW executive director, Amy Harmon; staff members Stephanie Beard and Norma Kennedy; board members Janet Tronc and Frank Souther; and board president Kathy Huff. The college hosted an informative tour of the campus and the area, as well as meetings with people at Lees-McRae who would be involved in starting a new site.

Early on, the expansion committee realized the need for help. I called upon a retired friend, Steve Langston, to see if he would be willing to consult with us. While dean at Georgia State University, he had opened new campuses at locations in other countries for Georgia State and was also knowledgeable of the New Opportunity School and Lees-McRae College. He agreed to spend several days with us in Berea at no charge except the cost of his plane ticket. The committee met with Steve for an entire day, and he led the group through the planning cycle for an expansion program. He insisted we design a matrix that would encompass every program aspect—and required us to think through why we offered every class, every social event, every field trip, and every internship experience. We learned so much about our own program in this process. All NOSW instructors provided a course outline and answered questions about how their course related to the mission of the New Opportunity School.

While Berea NOSW was working on our expansion plan and the legalities involved, Lees-McRae was working on the proposal to Kellogg. Leslie Carter, a Lees-McRae advancement officer, and Stephanie Keener worked hard to put together a realistic budget. Although the Berea program offers two sessions in summer and winter, realistically, Lees-McRae could offer only a summer session, as no housing would be available in winter. Also, the possibility of severe winter weather in Banner Elk, high in the mountains of North Carolina, could result in participants dropping out or the session being cancelled. We reminded ourselves that in the first two years at Berea, we held only summer sessions, and that it was actually a better plan for Lees-McRae to do so for the first few years.

Imagine the excitement at Lees-McRae and Berea when we learned the Kellogg Foundation was granting $50,000 to Lees-McRae College as start-up funds for a NOSW program. Stephanie Keener now held two jobs—directing both the Stephenson Center and the New Opportunity School. An old house on campus, near new residence halls, had been designated as the home of the Stephenson Center, and renovation was complete for office space for both programs. Ideally located, this house later became the focal point for NOSW participants. The small residence hall, built on the side of the mountain with a deck overlooking the flowing Elk River, was a perfect home away from home for participants. Stephanie put together an advisory board of local women interested in the program, and these and other volunteers made the single-occupancy rooms attractive homes for the three-week session. Amazingly, support came in from everywhere when word got out that the NOSW was coming to Lees-McRae. We received monetary donations, clothes for the clothing closet, offers to provide meals, and offers to teach classes. The support and excitement was most encouraging.

In July 2005, thirteen women arrived for the first class at our new expansion site. It was a special moment for me to meet these women who were making history. I listened carefully that first evening as they told their stories. These participants, like those we had been working with for many years in Kentucky, desired a better life for themselves and their families. That night, it was obvious to me that we had succeeded in expanding our NOSW program to help more Appalachian women. The Lees-McRae New Opportunity School program has now held eight sessions and graduated seventy-eight women and is becoming known all over North Carolina. There is no doubt that it will continue to succeed in the years ahead.

Carol Timblin, a graduate of Lees-McRae and a frequent contributor to *Our State* magazine, wrote a wonderful article about the Lees-McRae NOSW. I had the honor of appearing on Bill Friday's show, *North Carolina People*. Both the article and the TV program generated interest in the New Opportunity School across the state from women who learned the program could help them change their

NOSW graduation at Lees-McRae College, Banner Elk, North Carolina, July 2011. (© Michael Joslin)

lives, as well as from new donors and others in North Carolina eager to help the new site succeed.

The successful expansion at Lees-McRae College made those of us on the expansion committee well aware that we now had a model for growing more locations. We were fortunate to receive a grant from the Mary Reynolds Babcock Foundation in Winston-Salem, North Carolina, to hire an organizational management consultant, Kristin Lindsey. She reviewed our expansion efforts and made suggestions for us to consider for the futures of both sites. Her report was invaluable to all.

Meanwhile, we received several inquiries regarding possible expansion sites in other states. Janet Tronc and I made fact-finding trips to Maryville College in Tennessee and North Georgia College and State University in Dahlonega, Georgia. Both places had infrastructure that was perfect for our program but our primary concern was funding. Both locations had a lot of work to do before agreeing to become expansion sites. Unfortunately, for financial reasons, both locations have had to delay starting a NOSW. We hope more discussions will take place at a later date.

The Babcock Foundation awarded additional funds in 2009 to

One of the early graduating classes at Lees-McRae College in Banner Elk, North Carolina, the first expansion site for the NOSW which began in 2005. (© Michael Joslin)

hire a consultant, Tom Triplett, to "develop a structural model for NOSW going forward that will facilitate growth while maintaining consistency with NOSW's mission and guiding principles." Our expansion committee also felt the need for a process and criteria when examining new site possibilities and, most important, a governance structure. Tom was also asked to explore and develop a sustainable model for funding expansion sites as well as current ones. Program evaluation has always been of great importance at the Berea program, and Tom was also asked to explore tools to evaluate sites old and new.

Over several months, Tom made trips to both our North Carolina and Kentucky sites, and met with the expansion committee, board members, executive directors, and college officials at Lees-McRae. As Tom explored the governance of both sites, he defined the differences between a stand-alone organizational structure and a program operating under the auspices of a college with many levels of administrative control. The Berea NOSW has long been the "mother ship" as the founding location, and the efforts for expansion have originated within the board structure, particularly in the expansion committee. Tom's report in 2009 recommended the creation of a general "umbrella" governing board with 501(c)(3) nonprofit status not connected to the Berea NOSW. Although the members of the expansion committee of the Berea board of directors never complained about all the hard work involved, especially by committee chair, Janet Tronc, to go forward the governance structure would have to change. This umbrella board, which would ensure consistent and high-quality programs at current sites and new ones, could also provide central support services such as publicity, recruitment materials, fundraising development, and general help.

One of Tom's recommendations was to organize new programs at four-year higher education institutions. He preferred the more formal Lees-McRae model for several reasons: access to college faculty, staff, and facilities, ongoing financial and resource support, and name recognition of the host institution. By living in and becoming comfortable in a college campus environment, participants would be more likely to have the courage to enroll in college classes in the future.

Tom's report addressed the structure of an umbrella board and the need for a chief executive officer who would report directly to it. Board members would include at least two representatives from each NOSW site as well as "at large" members.

During fall 2009 and winter 2010, using Tom's report as a guide, the Berea board of directors under the leadership of Jay Ingle, president of the board, thoroughly explored Tom's report. At the January meeting of the Berea NOSW's board of directors, the board voted to "appoint three to five individuals to serve as initial directors of a 'new' umbrella board." Janet Tronc, Barbara Power, Mike Nichols, and I were appointed to represent the Berea board of directors. Tasks were assigned this new board, including recruiting and employing an executive director, beginning fundraising efforts, coordinating the transition process to the new model, and coordinating efforts required in forming a new nonprofit. The latter would require analysis of new structure, bylaws, incorporation, and additional legal document development.

The first organizational meeting of this new umbrella board took place in March 2010 and by August of that year, the new foundation was chartered in the state of Kentucky. During that year, officers of the new board were elected: chair, Janet Tronc; vice chair, Jane Stephenson; secretary, Diane Guelzow; and treasurer, Barbara Power. The two board members representing the Berea board were Mike Nichols and Barbara Power. Representing Lees-McRae were Diane Guelzow and Leslie Carter. Member-at-large was Virginia Underwood. Frank Taylor and Tim Marema were voted members-at-large at the July 2010 meeting. By November, a search committee had been formed and a job description written and approved for a director of this new organization.

It was a happy day in January 2011 when nonprofit status was granted by the IRS to the New Opportunity School for Women Foundation, Inc.

In May 2011, six candidates were interviewed by the search committee for the new part-time position directing our new foundation. The committee recommended by unanimous vote to hire Billy Newton to begin on June 1, 2011. The skills, education, and experience that Billy brought to the organization were a perfect match to our current needs. Billy, an ordained minister in the Presbyterian Church, U.S.A., had worked as a campus minister, director of several nonprofit organizations, and had grant-writing and fundraising experience.

Working from home in Maryville, Tennessee, Billy began visiting the two sites and learning about the NOSW. Billy enthusiastically began grant writing, organizing cultivation meetings with donors, and seeking the right location for our next expansion site.

Billy Newton is the President of the NOSW Foundation, the fundraising arm of the organization. The NOSW Foundation also looks for opportunities for new expansion sites. (© Mike Nichols)

In September 2011, Billy Newton and David Olive, president of Bluefield College, and members of his cabinet met to discuss the possibility of Bluefield as a site for a New Opportunity School. Located on the border of Virginia and West Virginia, Bluefield, a small Baptist liberal arts college, seemed an ideal location. I was pleased to join Billy on

# TWENTY-FIVE YEARS of HISTORY

Lansdell Hall on the campus of Bluefield College in Bluefield, Virginia, which will be the home of the NOSW's next expansion site opening in 2013. (© Staff, Bluefield College)

another trip a few weeks later, and after meeting the wonderfully caring administration and staff, we felt sure Bluefield was an ideal location. Many more meetings later, the NOSW foundation board enthusiastically agreed to issue an invitation to Bluefield College to become our third site. The first session is planned for May 2013.

During this same time period, changes continued to occur at both the Berea and Lees-McRae sites. After Amy Harmon decided to return to work at Berea College, Kim Gabbard (formerly Short), who had been with the NOSW for thirteen years, was made executive director. Norma Kennedy left to care for a very ill daughter. Jeneene Estridge was hired as a full-time development director. In 2007, both Kim and Jeneene resigned to pursue other careers and former board member Jan Gill, assumed the role of director a few months later. Jan immediately stepped in to plan our twentieth-year celebration

Executive Director of the NOSW at Lees-McRae College Karen Sabo, center, with graduates Meg Quinn, left, and Jess Stone. (© Meghan Wright)

to be held in November of that year. How exciting to celebrate with graduates, staff, instructors, donors, family, and friends our twenty years of changing lives. Those present will always remember our graduates standing on the stage at the end of the program singing *Lean on Me* while hugging each other and shedding a few tears.

Upon the resignation of Stephanie Keener as director of the Lees-McRae College NOSW, Lori Sliwa was selected as the next director. However, in 2009 Lori Sliwa resigned as director of the Lees-McRae program to join her husband as he began a new position at Maryville College. Carrie Guy was hired by Lees-McRae to take her place. In 2010, Jan Gill resigned as director of the Berea NOSW for personal reasons. At that time, the Berea board thought it a good time to evaluate the Berea program, especially when it came to job descriptions. I stepped in for a few months as interim director while

# TWENTY-FIVE YEARS of HISTORY

New Opportunity School for Women Founder Jane Stephenson and Executive Director Lori Sliwa console each other after their headquarters was burned in an arson fire in Berea, Kentucky, on December 12, 2011. (© David Stephenson)

a search progressed nationally for a new director. By April 2011, Lori Sliwa, former director of the Lees-McRae NOSW, was hired as the new executive director, bringing much experience and expertise from her two years heading the Lees-McRae program. Carrie Guy left the executive director position at Lees-McRae to go to graduate school, and Karen Sabo was selected to take her place. During all these changes, both programs continued efficiently, and successful sessions were held right on schedule. Recently, Cheryl Shippey was hired by Bluefield College to direct the new NOSW which will begin our third NOSW location in 2013.

December 12, 2011, will long be remembered as a dark day for the NOSW. In the early-morning hours, a fire destroyed the Berea NOSW office. The house we rented from the First Christian Church that had been home to the NOSW for fifteen years was gutted.

New Opportunity School for Women suffers an arson fire in Berea, Kentucky, on December 12, 2011. (© David Stephenson)

What a terrible experience to watch all the photographs, records, beautiful clothes in our clothing closet, desks, computers, personal belongings, quilts, furniture, and memorabilia of twenty-five years go up in flames. Later that day, the state fire marshall determined the cause: robbery and arson.

Three Lexington television stations, as well as reporters from the *Lexington Herald-Leader* and other media, arrived to film and write stories. Offers of desks, computers, clothing, and funds started pouring in. The First Christian Church came to our rescue immediately by offering space in their education building. Maxwell Street Presbyterian Church agreed to be a drop-off point in Lexington for donations until we could be in a new space and functioning again. More than a hundred people who had not previously known about our program sent donations and offers of equipment. Berea College students organized fundraising activities. My granddaughter's sixth-grade-class made posters, then solicited funds for us at a concert. Graduates posted on Facebook and dropped by to see the burned-out building and cry with us. E-mails poured in expressing sorrow and asking how they might help us. Most of all, we received heartfelt offers of support for us to continue. We were grateful that our work for low-income women was so supported and appreciated.

Everyone agreed that the fire, devastating as it was, would not stop the New Opportunity School from continuing to help Appalachian women. The staff worked tirelessly to keep the office open under very trying circumstances. Unfortunately, the winter session of 2012 had to be cancelled because most of the information pertaining to the session was lost in the fire and could not be replaced in time. It was several weeks before a new phone system was in place and refurbished computers donated by Berea College programmed. The greatest loss for most of us were the framed photos on our office wall. We hope that eventually, they can be replaced.

As of this writing, the arsonist has not been charged. Our location will continue in the First Christian Church. The 2012 summer session was held and all of the staff and our many friends agree that we have overcome this temporary setback. We are grateful for countless friends and donors who have made it possible for the NOSW to continue and thankful for a dedicated staff.

A bright spot in the middle of all this sadness was winning a contest sponsored by the national office of the American Association of Retired Persons. In summer 2011, I read in the AARP bulletin about a contest in which volunteers were asked to write in 1,000 words or less about their favorite charity. Well, that's not hard to do, I thought, as I sat at my computer and started writing. Seven entries would be chosen across the United States to win $5,000 for their special charity and then compete for an additional $10,000. We were so excited to learn we were selected as one of the $5,000 winners. We began telling and E-mailing everyone we knew to go online and cast a vote daily for the NOSW. Imagine our joy and grateful excitement when I received a phone call on November 1, telling me we had won the AARP final contest for a total of $15,000 for the NOSW.

Two days after the fire, a reception was held at Boone Tavern Hotel in Berea by the state office of the AARP. A check was presented to me and our staff, graduates, and friends who were present. How wonderful to have such a celebration of joy to erase the many tears shed over the fire. We are grateful to the many people who cast their vote for us every day for weeks.

As of this writing, 685 women have graduated from our three-week residential programs in Berea and at Lees-McRae College. The most inspiring part of this miracle is to behold the changes in the lives of our graduates. When people ask, "How can you possibly change a life in three weeks?" I can tell them that I have seen it happen time

The 2012 staff of NOSW—Berea, including (from left) Exectuive Director Lori Sliwa, Founder Jane Stephenson, Career/Education Counselor Stephanie Beard, and Office Manager Debbie King. (© Kara Beth Brunner)

after time, year after year. And our graduates tell us that as well. What we all have learned is that even a short-term intervention in a life can lead that person toward success. As one graduate said, "We had it in us all the time and didn't know it until they (the NOSW) pulled it out of us." I believe she is right. We believe in the women who come to our program. We love them. We accept them wherever they are in life—and help them move forward.

There are hundreds of success stories that could be told here. In fact, there are almost 700 because every woman who attended and completed a three-week session of the New Opportunity School has shown the courage and desire to seek a new life path. In ways large and small, changes have occurred and entire families have benefited. The women have found lasting friendships within their ranks and with the NOSW staff. In fact, they have become part of a sisterhood that is expressed in the poem on the next pages written by Jeff Blake after he attended a graduation.

I believe that the miracle of this program will continue, and more Appalachian women will seek our help and walk the courageous path to self-awareness and successful change through the New Opportunity School for Women.

May our many friends and supporters continue to walk with us on this journey of self-fulfillment for women all over our Appalachia, our country, and perhaps even the world as we continue for another twenty-five years.

## THE BUTTERFLY SISTERHOOD

Amazing, to me at least, how often the great mentors
and teachers of life are the common travelers
without pretense or guile who simply live,
wounds and all, with a kind of abandoned honesty.
They are moving beyond their fears and doubts
to a rugged kind of perseverance, an insistence
on a better life for themselves and their families.
They gave up long ago the silliness of mocking God
and instead are learning God is faithful
even in the hollows and valleys and mountains peaks
where they were born and quietly walk in dignity.
Such are the women I recently encountered
who call themselves The Butterfly Sisterhood.
They are the latest graduates of the New Opportunity School,
a place where women begin to walk, not limp or crawl,
and take control of their destinies.
They come as caterpillars and leave as butterflies,
thus the sisterhood they share as one.
It is in the darker places of their cocoons
where they are formed and begin to come to life.
They learn to dance like no one is watching.
A spirit of dance lifts them to a higher ground.
They put some spit-fire in their souls.
They go out singing hallelujah through an open door.
They learn the secret of never giving up on themselves.
They are inspired to learn again,
read again, write their own new journey
of hope and courage so all may celebrate their lives.
They say a loud, resounding *Yes* to who they are.
Saying *Yes I can* in a noisy world of No, turning obstacles
into nothing but golden opportunities.
Their daughters watch them with an awesome pride
and sing a chorus of *Go Mama Go*.
Their sons, strapping boys, drape their arms
over their mothers' shoulders and only smile.
They sing as one mighty earthly, heavenly choir,
*Your past is not your future!*
I tell you, no past ever is.
Fly, butterflies, fly.

– *Jeff Blake*

Graduates of the second class of the New Opportunity School for Women pose for a group photo in front of the President's home in Berea, Kentucky, in 1988. (© David Stephenson)

# Changing Lives in Appalachia

New Opportunity School graduates show their appreciation to founder Jane Stephenson in front of the President's home in Berea, Kentucky, in the summer of 1990. (© David Stephenson)

# APPENDIX

# Changing Lives in Appalachia

We thank the following graduates of the New Opportunity School for Women who willingly shared their stories. Those with an asterisk wished to remain anonymous.

| NAME | PROGRAM |
| --- | --- |
| Audrey Abner | Berea, winter, 2011 |
| Erin Asbury | Lees-McRae, summer, 2011 |
| Rose Marie Bailiff | Lees-McRae, summer, 2007 |
| Bobbie Boise | Berea, summer, 1989 |
| Vicky Lynn Bevis | Berea, winter, 2002 |
| Charlene Jean Bradford | Berea, winter, 2009 |
| Patricia Sue Sexton Hall | Berea, summer, 2003 |
| Jean Hardin | Berea, winter, 1999 |
| Chrissy Johns | Berea, Winter, 2011 |
| George Ann Lakes | Berea, summer, 1992 |
| Linda Baxter Linville | Berea, summer, 1988 |
| Sharon Malone | Lees-McRae, summer, 2007 |
| Mary Ann Morrison | Lees-McRae, summer, 2011 |
| Karen Morales | Berea, summer, 2008 |
| Marilyn Daneen Oakley | Lees-McRae, summer, 2010 |
| Katie Rollins | Berea, winter, 1991 |
| Lillian Pratt | Berea, winter, 2000 |
| Garnet Sexton | Berea, winter, 1991 |
| Marilyn Staton | Berea, winter, 2001 |
| Shirley Thompson | Berea, summer, 1988 |
| Peggy Wilson | Berea, summer, 1987 |
| Judy Williamson | Lees-McRae, summer, 2010 |
| *Alma | *Berea |
| *CJ | *Lees-McRae |
| *Dorothy | *Berea |
| *Mary | *Berea |
| *Sadie | *Berea |

# APPENDIX

## INFORMATION ABOUT BOOKS MENTIONED
### Appalachian Literature Books Used by NOSW

*Courageous Paths: Stories of Nine Appalachian Women* by Jane B. Stephenson, 1995. (Currently out of print but used copies are sometimes available at Amazon.com.)

*The Tall Woman* by Wilma Dykeman. (Originally published in 1962 by Wakestone Books.) Available at Jesse Stuart Foundation, 1645 Winchester Ave., Ashland, KY 41101 or online at jsfbooks.com.

*Kinfolks* by Gurney Norman. (Gnomon Press, 1977) Available on Amazon.com.

*Icy Sparks* by Gwyn Hyman Rubio. (Penguin, 1988). Available on Amazon.com and most bookstores.

### Other Books Mentioned

*Feel the Fear and Do It Anyway* by Susan Jeffers. (Fawcett Books, Random House, 1987). Available on Amazon.com.

*Negotiating a Perilous Empowerment: Appalachian Women's Literacies* by Erica Abrams Locklear. (Ohio University Press, 2011).

    Note: Through the years we have learned that often when participants of the NOSW return home, they are faced with family members who don't want to hear what they have learned. They may even be treated with hostility for having left their families and communities. There is often a fear by family and friends that what these women may have learned may eventually take them away from their home communities. This book addresses this issue in a broader context.

    Locklear, herself from Appalachia, writes about several Appalachian women as she helps the readers understand new literacies. She writes in her book: "...the skills and practices they use to gain knowledge—this is, new literacies—simultaneously empower and threaten the relationship they have with their home communities." She continues "...the long-held idea of Appalachia as an illiterate region—and residents' keen awareness of that label—sets Appalachian women's literacies apart as something worth exploring on their own." In an epilogue, Locklear recognizes the New Opportunity School for Women as a "real-life example of empowerment through new literacies." Available on Amazon.com.

## APPALACHIAN STATES

The following states have counties that are considered Appalachia. (All of West Virginia is designated Appalachia.)

List from the Appalachian Regional Commission, Washington, D.C. (See map and other statistical information about Appalachia at arc.gov.)

Alabama
Georgia
Kentucky
Maryland
Mississippi
New York
North Carolina
Ohio
Pennsylvania
South Carolina
Tennessee
Virginia
West Virginia

# APPENDIX

## CONTACT INFORMATION

NEW OPPORTUNITY SCHOOL, BEREA, KENTUCKY
Lori Sliwa, Executive Director
204 Chestnut Street
Berea, KY 40403
Phone: 859 985 7200
info@nosw.org
www.nosw.org

NEW OPPORTUNITY SCHOOL, LEES-McRAE COLLEGE
BANNER ELK, NORTH CAROLINA
Karen Sabo, Executive Director
The Stephenson Center
Post Office Box 218
Lees-McRae College
Banner Elk, NC 28604
Phone: 828 898 8905
sabok@lmc.edu
http://nosw.lmc.edu

NEW OPPORTUNITY SCHOOL FOUNDATION, INC.
Billy Newton, President
Post Office Box 6280
Maryville, TN 37802
Phone: 865 356 7400
www.nosfoundation.org
bnewton@nosw.org

## ABOUT the AUTHOR

Jane Stephenson was born and educated in the mountains of North Carolina. In 1966, soon after her marriage to Professor John Stephenson, they moved to Lexington, Kentucky, where they raised their three children. In 1984, Dr. Stephenson became President of Berea College. After the family moved to Berea, in 1987 Jane intensified her interest in educating adults by founding the nationally recognized New Opportunity School for Women, which celebrates its twenty-fifth anniversary this year. In addition to a NOSW site in Berea, another is also located in North Carolina and the third will open in May, 2013, in Bluefield, Virginia.

Jane has received numerous awards for her work with women, including Oprah's "Use Your Life Award" and more recently the AARP's "Create the Good" national award. She is the author of *Courageous Paths: The Stories of Nine Appalachian Women*.

Today, she divides her time between homes in Lexington, Kentucky, and Banner Elk, North Carolina, maintaining a life of active service to a wide variety of educational and cultural organizations.